100 ICONIC BUILDINGS TO SEE BEFORE YOU DIE

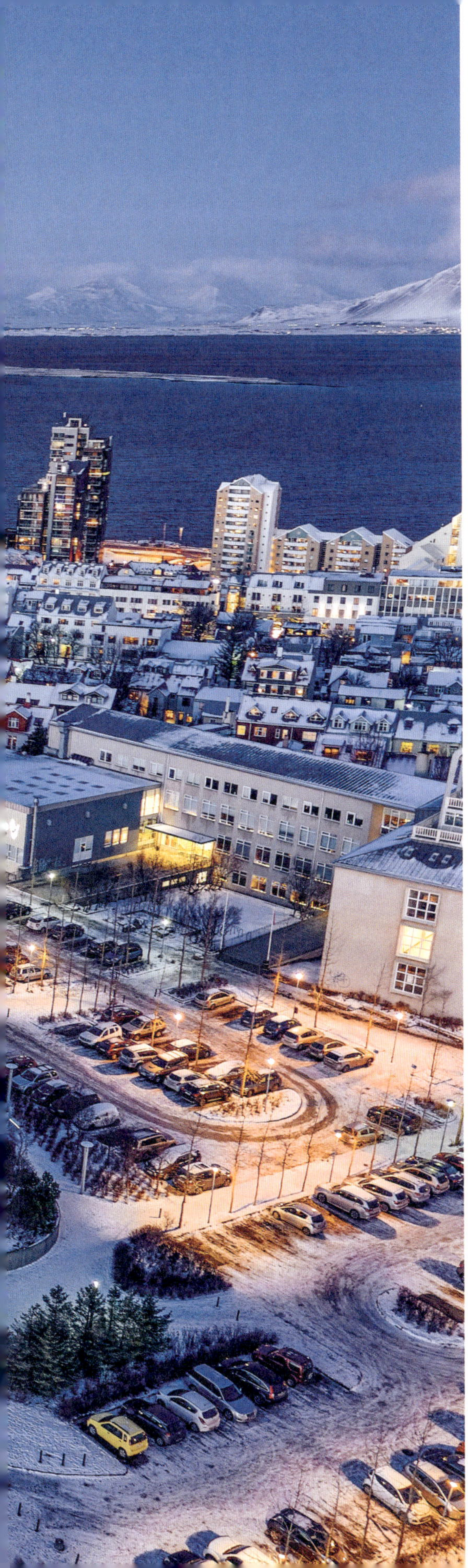

100 ICONIC BUILDINGS TO SEE BEFORE YOU DIE

CONTENTS

INTRODUCTION	8
EUROPE	
GEORGIAN BATH	12
PALACE OF WESTMINSTER	14
THE SHARD	16
SACRÉ-COEUR	17
NOTRE-DAME CATHEDRAL OF PARIS	20
EIFFEL TOWER	22
PALACE OF VERSAILLES	24
CHÂTEAUX OF THE LOIRE VALLEY	26
GREAT MOSQUE OF CÓRDOBA	28
ALHAMBRA	30
GAUDÍ'S BARCELONA	32
GUGGENHEIM MUSEUM	36
PENA PALACE	38
AMSTERDAM CANAL DISTRICT	40
NEUSCHWANSTEIN CASTLE	42
ELBPHILHARMONIE	44
BAUHAUS DESSAU	46
PALACE OF CULTURE AND SCIENCE	47
COLOSSEUM	50
PANTHEON	54
ST MARK'S BASILICA	56
RENAISSANCE FLORENCE	58
ST PETER'S	62
MILAN'S DUOMO	64
LEANING TOWER OF PISA	66
BRAN CASTLE	67
PARTHENON	70
HAGIA SOPHIA	72
KUNSTHAUS GRAZ	74
AMAGER BAKKE	75
BUDAPEST ART NOUVEAU	78
HALLGRÍMSKIRKJA	80
HEDDAL STAVE CHURCH	81

Previous page *Hallgrímskirkja, Reykjavík's iconic church*
Left *Paris's famous Eiffel Tower*

AFRICA AND THE MIDDLE EAST

THE MEDINA OF MARRAKESH	86
KSAR OF AÏT BENHADDOU	88
MAPUNGUBWE INTERPRETATION CENTRE	90
ZEITZ MOCAA	91
PYRAMIDS OF GIZA	94
KARNAK TEMPLE COMPLEX	98
PETRA	100
SHEIKH ZAYED GRAND MOSQUE	102
LOUVRE ABU DHABI	104
MUSEUM OF THE FUTURE	105
BURJ KHALIFA	108

ASIA

HEYDAR ALIYEV CENTRE	112
THE REGISTAN	114
CHANDIGARH	116
LOTUS TEMPLE	118
MEHRANGARH FORT	120
TAJ MAHAL	122
KHAJURAHO	126
GOLDEN TEMPLE OF AMRITSAR	128
MEENAKSHI TEMPLE	130
TIANJIN BINHAI LIBRARY	132
SHANGHAI TOWER	133
GREAT WALL OF CHINA	136
THE FORBIDDEN CITY	138
GYEONGBOKGUNG PALACE	142
TEMPLES OF KYOTO	144
HIMEJI CASTLE	148
NATIONAL ASSEMBLY BUILDING	150
ANGKOR WAT	152
GRAND PALACE	156
PETRONAS TOWERS	158
MARINA BAY SANDS	160
BOROBUDUR	162

OCEANIA

SYDNEY HARBOUR BRIDGE	166
SYDNEY OPERA HOUSE	168
MELBOURNE'S VICTORIAN ARCHITECTURE	170
BUNJIL PLACE	172
BELL TOWER	174
CARDBOARD CATHEDRAL	175
JEAN-MARIE TJIBAOU CULTURAL CENTRE	178

NORTH AMERICA

STATUE OF LIBERTY	182
EMPIRE STATE BUILDING	184
GUGGENHEIM MUSEUM	188
NEO-CLASSICAL WASHINGTON	190
GATEWAY ARCH	194
FALLINGWATER	195
THE CHICAGO SCHOOL	198
SEATTLE CENTER	200
GOLDEN GATE BRIDGE	202
HEARST CASTLE	204
WALT DISNEY CONCERT HALL	206
CLIFF PALACE, MESA VERDE	208
MIAMI ART DECO	210
CHÂTEAU FRONTENAC	214
CN TOWER	216
METROPOLITAN CATHEDRAL	217
MUSEO SOUMAYA	220
TEOTIHUACÁN	222
CHICHÉN ITZÁ	224

SOUTH AMERICA

CARTAGENA'S OLD TOWN	230
SANTUARIO DE LAS LAJAS	232
MACHU PICCHU	234
TEATRO AMAZONAS	238
BRASÍLIA	240
NITERÓI CONTEMPORARY ART MUSEUM	244
CASAPUEBLO	246
BAHÁ'Í TEMPLE OF SOUTH AMERICA	248

INDEX	250
ACKNOWLEDGMENTS	254

Right The three Pyramids of Giza, Egypt

Clockwise from left
Machu Picchu, an ancient citadel in Peru; the striking exterior of the Sydney Opera House; India's iconic Taj Mahal

INTRODUCTION

Machu Picchu. The Colosseum. Angkor Wat. The Sydney Opera House. These global landmarks top our bucket lists and appear on all our postcards and social media feeds. They're often our main reason for travelling, and the places we can't stop talking about when we get home. What do they all have in common? They're made by human hands, and we're here to show you the ones you absolutely can't miss.

After fierce debate among our team of travel experts (and we do mean fierce), we've decided upon the top 100 iconic buildings to see in a lifetime. Turn the pages and you'll discover epilogues of ancient empires, landmarks of some of our greatest cities and structures that kick-started architectural movements. Many are UNESCO World Heritage Sites, many have won awards and some are even Wonders of the World (both ancient and modern). Together, they span thousands and thousands of years, from the ruins of our ancient ancestors to the contemporary creations of pioneers shaping our world today.

Need more reason to seek out these icons? Just think: landmarks define entire cities, and even countries. What would New York City be without its iconic skyscraper, the Empire State Building? Can you picture Paris without its Eiffel Tower? How would you describe Egypt without its trio of pyramids? You can't. And that's what makes these buildings so legendary.

No doubt you'll recognize some of them – places like Petra and the Taj Mahal have hardly gone under the radar – but there may be some surprises, too. How about a fairytale-esque cathedral in an isolated region of Colombia? Or a dazzling government building in overlooked Bangladesh? You might also spot a statue, a bridge or a certain great wall here and there; they're not technically buildings, but we still made them, and we think they deserve a place on the list.

This is our top 100, and every entry is special. Tick off just one, and you're guaranteed a travel experience that'll stay with you forever. Tick off them all... well, we'll just have to make another list.

EUROPE

Europe's architecture was iconic from the very beginning. A couple of thousand years ago, master builders from the ancient Greek and Roman empires constructed some of the world's greatest buildings – so great that they still stand strong today. Since then, the continent has witnessed waves of rulers (the Habsburgs, the Medicis, the Soviets), who paraded their power through extravagant architecture and left hulking palaces and government buildings in their wake. But Europe has also been influenced by its great artists and architects. The Renaissance movement may have started in Florence, but numerous cities fell under its spell; Art Nouveau was equally enchanting, and examples of the style can be found throughout the continent; and then there was Bauhaus, the quietly cool German school that offered architects something totally different. Europe embraced it all.

Clockwise from left The townhouses of the Circus; Pulteney Bridge, which appeared in the scene of Javert's suicide in Les Misérables; Bath during autumn

BATH · UK

GEORGIAN BATH

WHERE Bath's centre features the best examples
TRANSPORT Trains to Bath Spa station run from Bristol and London Paddington

Nowhere does 18th-century architecture quite like Bath. This Georgian gem is a treasure trove of honey-stone terraces, arched bridges and stately parks – many of which have changed little since Jane Austen strolled through this city.

Period dramas can't get enough of Bath. This Georgian city has been a backdrop for numerous TV shows and films. Spot it in regency romance *Bridgerton*; look closely and you'll see the Pulteney Bridge pretending to be French in 2012's *Les Misérables*; and, inevitably, it's appeared in a few Jane Austen adaptations (the author lived here), most recently 2022's love-it-or-hate-it *Persuasion*.

So, why all the screen time? Not only is Bath beautiful, it's also incredibly well preserved. This is the UK's most impressive collection of Georgian architecture, with a staggering 5,000 listed buildings (and this isn't a big city). Take a walk around its centre and you'll quickly come across columned townhouses, swoon-worthy circuses and golden-stoned churches. It all feels built to be beautiful, and it was.

Bath has been a spa since Roman times, and the foundations of the original Roman Baths are still a major tourist attraction. But it was in the Georgian era (after prominent physician Thomas Guidott set up a hydrotherapy practice around its hot springs) that it became one of the most fashionable destinations in England – and got a makeover to match. Grand homes and guest houses were hewn from honey-hued limestone, fronted with Palladian columns and linked by elegant footways like Pulteney Bridge. Architects John Wood, the Elder and his son John Wood, the Younger, were largely to thank for the city's new look, and happily, much of their work remains today. Modern shops, cool bars and edgy restaurants may have moved in, but their façades are still Georgian ("Phew", say the location scouts).

MUST-SEE BUILDINGS

ROYAL CRESCENT
This arc of 30 terraced townhouses with perfectly proportioned columns and balconettes is as impressive today as it would have been to its famous former residents.

THE CIRCUS
This ring of residences was modelled on ancient monuments: its diameter mimics that of Stonehenge and its circular design was inspired by Rome's Colosseum *(p50)*.

HOLBURNE MUSEUM
Eagle-eyed *Bridgerton* fans will recognize the colonnaded façade of this historic art gallery as the setting for Lady Danbury's house *(Great Pulteney St)*.

PULTENEY BRIDGE
This Palladian bridge overlooks a tumbling weir and is one of only four bridges in the world to have shops spanning its full length on both sides.

PARADE GARDENS
Overlooking the River Avon, this Georgian pleasure garden is one of the city's most attractive parks, with manicured lawns.

EUROPE   13

LONDON · UK

PALACE OF WESTMINSTER

WHERE Parliament Square, Westminster **TRANSPORT** Westminster tube is the nearest station **INFORMATION** Palace tours run on Sat all year, plus Mon–Fri during parliament's summer recess; ticket required (parliament.uk/visiting)

A grand statement of the lofty ideals of the Victorian age, the UK's Houses of Parliament is a Gothic Revival masterpiece. It's a setting every bit as dramatic as the febrile political intrigue that takes place within.

Spread out magisterially along the north bank of the River Thames, the Palace of Westminster is a symphony in stone. Extravagant tracery adorns the honey-coloured façade, and arched windows arrow up towards turrets and pinnacles, capped by finials that pierce the sky. Dominating the spectacle, the Elizabeth Tower – home to Big Ben, the Great Bell – presides over London like a time-keeping sentinel.

A LINK WITH THE PAST

The apogee of Neo-Gothic, the palace is such a familiar landmark on London's skyline that it's strange to think it could have taken a very different form. When its medieval predecessor was gutted by a colossal fire in 1834, many argued its replacement should be Classical in style, the vogue of the time. The result was a hybrid: Classical in symmetry, yet dressed in a profusion of Gothic detail in ode to the era's idealized vision of Britain's medieval past.

Visitors will certainly feel humbled by history stepping into the 11th-century Westminster Hall, starting point for tours and one of the few parts of the palace to survive the great fire of 1834. Scenes of both beauty and brutality have played out under its hammer-beam roof, from royal coronation banquets to the grisly trials of Guy Fawkes and Charles I.

From the far end of the medieval hall, steps lead up into the 19th-century palace, the old merging with the new: a wealth of carved wood, statuary, stained glass and painting. It's a thrill to enter the House of Commons, its green-baize benches the familiar backdrop to fiery political debate, yet it pales in brilliance next to the crimson-clad House of Lords and its gilded Sovereign's throne. It's a reminder that this is still, in part, a royal palace.

Past and present live side by side in the Palace of Westminster, yet its future is uncertain. With renovation needed, MPs have voted to up sticks to allow repairs to go ahead. Whether the move is temporary or permanent, the palace will endure – a powerful symbol of London and a nation's 19th-century vigour.

The Palace of Westminster, the seat of the two Houses of Parliament for almost 500 years

LONDON · UK

THE SHARD

WHERE 32 London Bridge St **TRANSPORT** London Bridge is the nearest train and tube station **INFORMATION** Viewing platforms open 10am–10pm; ticket required (the-shard.com)

Rising above the London skyline and reflecting the city in its façade, this striking shard of glass is a modern icon. It's also the UK's – and Western Europe's – tallest building.

London isn't short of iconic architecture, and over the years, the city has been defined by its buildings. The Tower of London cast a shadow over the Thames during the medieval era; then the domed St Paul's Cathedral rose to become a centre of religious and social life; and later, the stately Elizabeth Tower became, probably, the world's most famous clock tower. But then the Shard arrived. *The* symbol of modern London, this lofty skyscraper tops out at just over 300 m (1,000 ft) tall. With its steel-and-glass façade and iconoclastic "broken" spire, it's a thoroughly modern building (built between 2009 and 2012), but one that harks back to historic London – it was designed to resemble the church spires of old, as well as the masts of trading ships that once plied the Thames.

Conceived by architect Renzo Piano, the Shard drew attention not only for its striking design, but for its revolutionary top-down construction – work began on the upper tower while the basement was being excavated. It was conceived as a "vertical city", and today it encompasses all realms of 21st-century London life (private apartments, offices, restaurants and bars). But for most visitors, it's all about the viewing platforms. Fly up to the 69th and 72nd floors – by far the city's highest vantage points – and you'll find yourself looking down, and down, and down at all those other icons.

Right The glassy Shard, towering over central London

16 EUROPE

PARIS · FRANCE

SACRÉ-CŒUR

WHERE 35 Rue du Chevalier de la Barre **TRANSPORT** Abbesses (metro) is the nearest station; the Montmartre funicular runs to the foot of the building **INFORMATION** Open 6:30am–10:30pm Mon–Sun; entry is free (sacre-coeur-montmartre.com)

Situated atop Montmartre hill, the spectacular white basilica of the Sacré-Cœur watches over Paris from one of the city's highest points. It's famed for both its design – its trio of Neo-Byzantine towers is unique in Paris – and its epic views.

It takes hard work to reach the Sacré-Cœur (the "Sacred Heart"): over 200 steps stretch from the gardens underneath to the foot of the basilica. Although you can shorten the trip by jumping on the speedy funicular, there is value in the slower ascent – step by step, the immensity of the building comes into view. And what a view. Sporting a trio of Romano-Byzantine towers and an 84-m (276-ft)-high bell tower, this white-stone basilica casts a surprising silhouette over the city – and it's been that way for over a century.

Conceived in the aftermath of the Franco-Prussian War and the bloody suppression of the Paris Commune (a short-lived socialist government), the Sacré-Cœur was framed as a bulwark against secularism and revolutionary unrest – and the building remains controversial among some Parisians today. Construction began in 1875, following the designs of French architect Paul Abadie (who envisioned the basilica's striking Romano-Byzantine style), and took around 40 years to build.

Today, many head here simply for the panorama: from the steps outside, the City of Lights unfurls before you. But don't forget to venture inside, too. As you walk into the cool nave, lined with flickering candles and alive with hushed prayers, you'll be struck by the huge mosaics and stained-glass windows. The Sacré-Cœur's exterior may be unique in Paris, and its panorama may be popular, but this colourful inner sanctuary might just be its most beautiful view.

PHOTO OPPORTUNITY

Fancy an even better view of Paris, and even more stairs? You can climb another 280 steps to the top of the Sacré-Cœur's dome, where a 360-degree view of the French capital awaits.

Next page The Romano-Byzantine towers of the Sacré-Cœur

The west façade of the cathedral, with its central rose window

PARIS · FRANCE

NOTRE-DAME CATHEDRAL OF PARIS

WHERE 6 Parvis Notre-Dame – Place Jean-Paul II **TRANSPORT** Saint-Michel Notre-Dame (RER) and Cité (metro) are the nearest stations **INFORMATION** Open 7:50am–7pm Mon–Wed & Fri, 7:50am–10pm Thu, 8:15am–7:30pm Sat–Sun (notredamedeparis.fr)

No other building is more associated with the history of Paris than Notre-Dame. This Gothic monument has commanded the capital's skyline for close to a millennium, and come rain or shine (or fire), it continues to do so today.

Who's the main character on the Parisian skyline? You might say the famous Eiffel Tower or the more unusual Sacré-Cœur, but long before these icons made their marks, another dame ruled the roost. She has a spire that reaches for the sky, massive twin bell towers, gleaming rose windows and terrifying gargoyles that guard her ledges. Meet Notre-Dame Cathedral: the protagonist of Paris's story for close to nine centuries.

The history of Notre-Dame can be traced back nearly 900 years, when construction began under the direction of Bishop Maurice de Sully in 1163. Intended to reflect the growing power of the Catholic Church and the importance of Paris as a political and religious centre, the cathedral was no small monument. This was Gothic architecture at its most intimidating: built over two centuries (it opened in 1345), fit for up to 6,000 people and adorned with a city's worth of statues (some good – apostles and angels – some bad – chimeras and flesh-eating strixes).

For centuries, Notre-Dame stood at the heart of Parisian life, from holding religious feasts to providing the backdrop to political events, including Napoleon Bonaparte's coronation in 1804. A few years later, in 1831, French author Victor Hugo wrote adoringly about the cathedral, putting it front and centre of his acclaimed novel *The Hunchback of Notre-Dame*.

A DEVASTATING FIRE

It is easy to imagine Hugo despairing at the building going up in flames on a spring evening in 2019, nearly two centuries after he depicted the cathedral with such passion. The blaze severely damaged Notre-Dame, notably causing the collapse of the spire, but the disaster sparked an outpouring of support and a major restoration effort was launched; in December 2024, Notre-Dame finally reopened.

Today, the cathedral stands again in all her glory, formidable on the French skyline, but inside she's a gentle giant. Kaleidoscopic rose windows fill the central nave with shafts of colourful light, elegant sculptures are dotted around and the soft hum of prayers fills the echoing interior. Sit in a pew for a moment and you'll see why Hugo loved her so.

The Eiffel Tower, the tallest structure in Paris

PARIS · FRANCE

EIFFEL TOWER

WHERE Avenue Gustave Eiffel **TRANSPORT** Champ de Mars – Tour Eiffel (RER) and Bir-Hakeim (metro) are the nearest stations **INFORMATION** Open Jul–Aug: 8:45am–11:45pm Mon–Sun; Sep–June: 9:15am–10:45pm Mon–Sun; ticket required (toureiffel.paris/en)

If you had to sum up Paris in a shape, you'd probably draw the Eiffel Tower. An engineering masterpiece when it first graced the skyline, this wrought-iron monument has defined the City of Lights ever since.

The Eiffel Tower will accompany you everywhere you go in the French capital. You'll see it on fridge magnets in souvenir shops, spot it lurking in the background of paintings on the walls of old brasseries or, better yet, glimpse its spire peeping through gaps in the city's streetscape. There is no doubt the tower has become the symbol of Paris. In fact, the Iron Lady reminds the city of her presence every night, when the rotating beam at the summit of the tower sweeps the Parisian horizon.

A REVOLUTIONARY

It might feel like the Eiffel Tower has always been there, silently watching over the city, but it was built less than 150 years ago. Designed to be a temporary entrance arch for the 1889 Exposition Universelle (World Fair) in Paris, the wrought-iron lattice tower was the world's tallest structure at the time and a showcase of France's industrial prowess. Locals weren't very impressed: the building was met with furious criticism from Paris's artists and intellectuals, with some going so far as to describe it as a "useless and monstrous tower".

Opposition to the building didn't last long, however. Instead of disassembling the structure at the end of its lease in 1910, Paris City Hall agreed to keep the tower – largely because it had proved its worth as an experimental antenna for radio transmissions.

Today, it's more of a tourist attraction than a transmitter. You can climb all the way to the top or simply survey it from ground level, admiring the tens of thousands of iron lattices intertwining with mesmerizing geometry.

PHOTO OPPORTUNITY

Every hour on the hour, once the sun sets and for five short minutes, the Eiffel Tower puts on a coat of sparkling lights. Watch the iconic sight from the Trocadéro Esplanade for the best photos.

Clockwise from top The palace's grand façade; its landscaped gardens; the Hall of Mirrors

VERSAILLES · FRANCE

PALACE OF VERSAILLES

WHERE Place d'Armes **TRANSPORT** Versailles Château Rive Gauche train station **INFORMATION** Open Apr–Oct: 9am–6:30pm Tue–Sun; Nov–Mar: 9am–5:30pm Tue–Sun; ticket required, but the gardens are free (en.chateauversailles.fr)

The extravagant Palace of Versailles was built with one goal: to showcase the extent of the French king's riches and power. Walk its lofty halls and landscaped gardens and you'll quickly realize he wasn't short of cash.

If you want to gawp at how the other half live, there's no better place than this. The Palace of Versailles is one of the most spectacular royal residences in the world, and it's overwhelming in more ways than one. Firstly, it's huge; this is one of the largest palaces in Europe, hosting 2,300 rooms and once housing up to 20,000 people. Secondly, the site cost an unimaginable amount to build (estimates in today's money vary wildly but are always upwards of $2 billion, sometimes up to $300 billion). And lastly, it's one of the world's most visited historic places, with 10 million visitors a year.

Turn up on the site four centuries or so ago, though, and the story was quite different. Versailles was originally a modest hunting lodge until Louis XIV, also known as the Sun King, set his eyes upon it. Beginning in 1661, and with the help of the finest Baroque architects, artists and landscape designers, the French king transformed the lodge into a lavish royal palace. For the next century, Versailles became the stage of political affairs, aristocratic love games and royal festivities.

Today, the atmosphere isn't quite the same – tour groups and snap-happy visitors have taken over – but the setting is still as opulent. Walk through the gardens and you'll immediately notice the perfect symmetry of the site: designed by landscaper André Le Nôtre, the park's lanes, hedges and pools stretch over hundreds of hectares in impeccably mirrored patterns with near-mathematical elegance.

More symmetry awaits on the palace's imposing façade, where Classical columns, statues of mythological figures and intricate gold finishings shimmer in the sun. But there's even more drama inside. At every turn, you'll stand in awe of the abundance of marble panelling, gilded mouldings and painted ceilings. The Hall of Mirrors is a particular highlight – here 357 mirrors reflect the light from towering windows. Then there are Louis XIV's ornate apartments, where 100 members of the court would gather daily to attend the king's getting-up and going-to-bed ceremonies. Spare a thought for them: Louis XIV ruled for a near-endless 72 years and 102 days.

MORE LIKE THIS

Schönbrunn Palace, Austria
This stunning Baroque residence served as the summer home of the Habsburg imperial family. Magnificent interiors and extensive gardens reflected the wealth and power of the Austrian monarchy.

Zwinger Palace, Germany
Another masterpiece of Baroque architecture, Zwinger Palace was designed as a setting for court festivities, tournaments and exhibitions. It now houses several museums, including the Old Masters Picture Gallery and the Porcelain Collection.

LOIRE VALLEY · FRANCE

CHÂTEAUX OF THE LOIRE VALLEY

WHERE Examples can be found in Pays de la Loire and Centre-Val de Loire **TRANSPORT** Tours and Amboise are the nearest railway stations **INFORMATION** Hours and admission charges vary; for details, see regional tourism website (loirevalley-france.co.uk)

Fan of fairytales? Venture to the Loire Valley and you'll discover a land of towers and turrets (though sadly no magical beings). Once home to France's royals, this scenic area features over 300 stunning castles and palaces.

It's hard to pick a favourite. Located in the heart of France, the stunning Loire Valley hosts hundreds of fairytale castles and swoon-worthy palaces. And they're all different: some have moats, drum towers and fortified walls, while others feature vast landscaped gardens and façades so fancy it's hard to believe they were just people's homes. But no ordinary people, of course.

Before the French royal court moved to Paris, the country's nobility largely lived in the Loire Valley, the so-called Garden of France. This lush corner of the country was famed for its fruit orchards, sweeping vineyards and historic towns – and, perhaps most importantly, it was close to the royal seat of Tours. From the Middle Ages, royals and royal wannabes began to move in, building grand estates along the banks of the River Loire. The good life didn't last forever, however. In 1528, King Francis I transferred the monarchy back to Paris, and the nobles were forced to follow suit. Still, despite being neglected for centuries, looted during the French Revolution and commandeered by the military during both world wars, most of the châteaux are still standing today.

NO ORDINARY CHÂTEAUX

The Loire Valley châteaux didn't start off so extravagant, though they were always rather grand. Early examples include boxy, medieval-looking structures, complete with drawbridges and turrets (some of which were built during the Hundred Years' War and later renovated by royals). But as the years went on, and the Italian Renaissance began to inspire the country's architects, ostentation prevailed. Defensive features were dialled down in favour of flamboyant decorations: double-helix staircases, sumptuous frescoes, huge tapestries, lavish gardens... the list goes on.

Want to go house-hunting? The 280-km (174-mile) Loire Valley is located between Chalonnes-sur-Loire and Sully-sur-Loire, and happily, many of the most magnificent châteaux are in close proximity to one another. You could hire a bike to castle-hop, or take to the skies on a hot-air balloon ride above the valley. The latter feels a little more royal.

MUST-SEE BUILDINGS

LANGEAIS
Rebuilt in the 1460s but still incorporating historic elements (like the remains of a 10th-century keep), Langeais is an icon of the Loire. Its drawbridge and carved fireplace are particular highlights *(Pl Pierre de Brosse)*.

CHÂTEAU D'AMBOISE
Built in the 15th century, this is France's first Italianate-style palace *(Montée de l'Emir Abd El Kader)*.

CHÂTEAU DE CHENONCEAU
Spanning the river in an imaginative engineering move, this château is famed for its gardens *(37150 Chenonceaux)*.

CHÂTEAU DE CHAMBORD
Breathtakingly grand, the largest château in the Loire is famed for its lavish interior décor *(41250 Chambord)*.

Clockwise from top
The mighty Château de Chambord; elegant Château d'Amboise; Château de Chenonceau, which features a unique bridge over the river

Clockwise from top
The Mosque-Cathedral, scenically situated by the River Guadalquivir; the bell tower (once the site of a minaret); the hypostyle hall

CÓRDOBA · SPAIN

GREAT MOSQUE OF CÓRDOBA

WHERE Calle Cardenal Herrero 1 **TRANSPORT** Walk or taxi from Córdoba train station or Córdoba bus station **INFORMATION** Open Mar–Oct: 10am–7pm Mon–Sat, 8:30am–7pm Sun; Nov–Feb: 8:30am–6pm daily; ticket required (mezquita-catedraldecordoba.es)

Have you ever seen a mosque like this? Featuring an opulent mihrab, a striking minaret and a Renaissance cathedral, Córdoba's Great Mosque is an architectural hybrid, fusing Islamic and Christian elements to breathtaking effect.

Let's start at the very beginning. The Great Mosque of Córdoba, also known as the Mosque-Cathedral of Córdoba or simply the Mezquita, was founded in the 8th century – while Andalucía was under Islamic rule – and built on the site of an earlier Visigothic church. The original building is a masterclass in Islamic architecture, famed for its airy rooms, courtyard lined with orange trees and iconic horseshoe arches. The latter take pride of place in the striking hypostyle hall, which features seemingly endless rows of 856 columns, above which rise two-tiered, red-and-white arches. The mosque was expanded several times over the centuries, with additions only making it more lavish: spot intricate mosaics, stucco carvings and gleaming gold tesserae.

Everything changed after the Siege of Córdoba (1236), when power shifted to the Christian King Ferdinand III of Castile. The mosque became, in essence, a cathedral, and its lofty minaret was converted into a bell tower. But it wasn't until the 16th century when, in a remarkable feat of engineering, a Gothic nave, transept and choir were inserted into its centre. This part of the building feels like another world, with soaring Gothic arches, a ribbed vaulted ceiling and a feast of Mannerist embellishments. It's spectacular and still manages to hold its own in a building that's hardly lacking in spectacle.

WHEN TO GO

In late March or early April, Córdoba marks Holy Week with solemn Catholic processions and services. In May, Córdoba's many private and public courtyards are bedecked with plants and flowers for the Fiesta de los Patios (Patio Festival).

EUROPE

Clockwise from left Palacio del Partal; the Court of Lions; the sprawling Alhambra site

10

GRANADA · SPAIN

ALHAMBRA

WHERE Calle Real de la Alhambra **TRANSPORT** Reach by taxi or private vehicle **INFORMATION** Open Apr–Oct: 8:30am–8pm & 10–11:30pm; Nov–Mar 8:30am–6pm & 8–9:30pm; ticket required (alhambradegranada.org)

You can't go to Granada without visiting the Alhambra. Set against the snow-tipped Sierra Nevada mountains, this fortified medieval palace is one of the most iconic monuments of Islamic architecture, not only in Spain, but in the world.

The Alhambra began as a dream, sketched into the dirt on Sabika Hill by Emir Muhammad Ibn Al-Ahmar. The 13th-century founder of the Nasrid dynasty and ruler of the Muslim Emirate of Granada, Al-Ahmar imagined a great palace to suit his equally great dynasty. It's safe to say he got it: the Alhambra was built on that very hill and Al-Ahmar's dynasty was the longest lived in the Iberian Peninsula.

But it didn't last forever. In the 1810s and 1820s, the site was damaged by Napoleonic forces, plus an earthquake, and fell into disrepair. It later attracted European Romantics, who were inspired by the building's elegant decay and brought worldwide attention to the site. Restoration work quickly ensued.

BUILT TO IMPRESS

If you spotted the vast walls of the Alhambra, sprawled across a hefty hilltop, you might think twice about invading. That was the idea. Built from rammed earth that was reddish in colour – hence the name, derived from the Arabic for red – and fortified with ramparts and a 26-m (85-ft) command tower, the Torre del Homenaje, the palace was a formidable sight. It was well thought out beyond its defensive abilities, too. Water, essential in the area's dry summers, came from the river below via a nifty series of aqueducts and water channels.

But it wasn't all practical. Al-Ahmar's vast palace was a showcase of his dynasty's wealth, and he didn't hold back when it came to décor. Few walls are plain here; spot colourful tiles, wood carving and ornamental stucco featuring calligraphic and floral designs at every turn. Lush gardens and mirror-like pools also abound. It can feel overwhelming, so focus on the best parts. The Generalife (once the country estate of Nasrid kings) is beloved for its neat gardens, while the Palacio del Partal is considered the oldest surviving building in the Alhambra complex. And then there's the 14th-century Court of the Lions (named after the stone lions surrounding its central fountain). Considered a perfect example of Nasrid architecture, this palace hosts graceful archways and vaulted ceilings embellished with elaborate *muqarnas*, three-dimensional stucco decorations. Few buildings compare.

PHOTO OPPORTUNITY

It's far too easy to fill your camera roll in the Alhambra, but don't miss photographing the Court of Lions. For the best pictures, aim your camera through the pillars and slightly up. A good quality zoom lens will help you record details of the *muqarnas* that, from floor level, you may miss.

The Sagrada Família, still undergoing construction

BARCELONA · SPAIN

GAUDÍ'S BARCELONA

WHERE Throughout Barcelona, with many examples in the Eixample district
TRANSPORT Taxis run from Barcelona Sants train station or Barcelona-El Prat airport to the city centre; a shuttle bus also runs from the airport

All cities have their famous locals, but few end up shaping a place like Antoni Gaudí has Barcelona. A true visionary, his enduring legacy shines in reptilian rooftops, pick 'n' mix façades and candy-cane spires around the Catalan capital.

You can't speak about Barcelona without mentioning Gaudí, arguably one of the world's pioneering architects. During his career, the Spaniard etched his own architectural language into buildings across the city he called home from 1868. A devout Catholic, Gaudí saw nature as the highest expression of God's work and was inspired by organic forms, blending them with his faith and Catalan heritage. The result was an absence of straight lines or sharp edges, a stark departure from the era's norms that shook up the establishment and still causes controversy.

THE ETERNAL TEMPLE

There are around 12 Gaudí creations in Barcelona, and perhaps the most famous of all is the Sagrada Família. Instantly recognizable with its quirky masonry and porcupine roof, it's probably best known for taking over 140 years to build, having started in 1882. When it's finally completed, over a century will have passed since Gaudí's death in 1926.

Sat in the heart of Eixample, a district famous for its gridded street design and chamfered corners, the zany church rockets into the sky with over a dozen spires. Its three stonework façades depict different moments from the Bible, although the nativity scene, so embellished it seems like it's melting, was the only one completed during Gaudí's lifetime. Inside, it's impossible not to stumble looking up in the church's nave, its mighty columns and spiny roof akin to an abstract rainforest canopy. Add to this the technicolour light streaming through big stained-glass windows and it's hard not to be mesmerized.

MODERNISM MEETS NATURE

Both before and during the construction of the Sagrada Família, Gaudí was gaining wider recognition within Barcelona and beyond. He particularly caught the attention of Spanish entrepreneur Eusebi Güell, who began commissioning him to create some of the masterpieces we know today. One such piece was Park Güell, intended by its namesake to be a garden city for Barcelona's wealthy families. The idea never quite came to fruition, but sometimes the best things come from waylaid plans: the fanciful park that was completed in 1914 showcases the best of Gaudí's meticulous craftwork. Take the Casa del Guarda near the entrance, a gatehouse seemingly whittled out of gingerbread and iced with a wonky white roof. Or the twin staircase, home to a technicolour salamander that's become Park Güell's de facto emblem. You could easily spend hours upon hours here, pouring over the tiny details in the park's upcycled trencadís mosaics.

A LIFETIME CREATING

While every Gaudí creation is unique, what unites them all is their skill and romanticism, and Casa Vicens, Gaudí's first major commission, has both in abundance. Its mesmerizing checkerboard façade is an explosion of colour, at once austere and flamboyant, fusing Moorish Revivalism and Islamic art. Inside, sgraffito floral motifs point to an obsession with nature that became one of Gaudí's trademarks. Another Gaudí trademark? There being something delightful in every nook, as is the case with Casa Milà, better known as La Pedrera. There isn't a single straight line in this apartment building (the last private residence to be designed by Gaudí); the façade ripples like water, all undulating surfaces, wrought iron and odd-shaped windows. The attic is perhaps the most impressive feature, comprising 270 parabolic vaults and a Catalan arched ceiling; wandering in here feels like you've been swallowed by a mythical sea creature. On the rooftop, strange hydra-headed chimneys stare you down and ventilation shafts have been moulded into shapes that look like giant scoops of ice cream. From here, in the distance, Sagrada Família's iconic spires wave back, as if signalling Gaudí's everlasting influence on Barcelona.

PHOTO OPPORTUNITY

Plaça de Gaudí, beside the Sagrada Família, is the perfect place to pap the iconic church in all its glory. Facing the nativity façade, you might even be lucky enough to get a shot of the building's reflection shimmering in the park's pond.

Clockwise from right
Exploring the undulating roof of La Pedrera; Park Güell, representing Gaudí's fanciful style; Casa Batlló's roof rippling like a dragon in flight

MUST-SEE BUILDINGS

SAGRADA FAMÍLIA
Barcelona's most visited sight, this church is the city's unofficial emblem *(Carrer de Mallorca, 401)*.

CASA VICENS
Gaudí's first major project features vibrant geometric patterns that blend with its gardens *(Carrer de les Carolines, 20–26)*.

CASA BATLLÓ
With its dragon-scaled roof and chameleon-like chimneys, Casa Batlló is a prime example of Gaudí incorporating the natural world into his designs *(Passeig de Gràcia, 43)*.

LA PEDRERA
Finished in 1912, this building raised eyebrows in its time due to its undulating stone façade and abstract roof sculptures *(Passeig de Gràcia, 92)*.

PARK GÜELL
Part of Gaudí's naturalist phase, this park represents his fanciful style. It opened to the public in 1926, the year of Gaudí's death *(Carrer d'Olot, 7)*.

Clockwise from left The curves up close; the 9-m (30-ft) *Maman*; the titanium sails reflected in the water

BILBAO · SPAIN

GUGGENHEIM MUSEUM

WHERE Abandoibarra Etorb, 2, Abando **TRANSPORT** Abando Indalecio Prieto (train) or the Guggenheim (tram) are the nearest stations **INFORMATION** Open 10am–7pm Tue–Sun (to 8pm Thu); ticket required (guggenheim-bilbao.eus)

It's not often that an art gallery changes the fortunes of an entire city, but the Guggenheim is no ordinary art gallery: it's a twisting, shimmering knot of titanium and glass, nestled in Bilbao's estuary.

If one building defines Bilbao, it's the Guggenheim. Built in 1997 by Canadian-American architect Frank Gehry in the style that would later become his trademark, it consists of stacks of asymmetrical layers resembling bent sheets of metal. Gehry was already a world-famous architect by this time, his curving buildings often likened to the work of Pablo Picasso, but the Guggenheim raised the bar – not just for his own work, but for the whole world of museum design.

Perched on a bend of the Nervión river, the building resembles a flower from above and a gravity-defying ship of liquid mercury from the side. The psychedelic atmosphere is only enhanced by the sculptures that sit in its grounds: *Maman*, a towering metal spider by the sculptor Louise Bourgeois, and *Puppy*, a West Highland terrier by the artist Jeff Koons. Inside, the curving walls create a disorientating effect, like you're standing in a hall of mirrors. Gehry has often described his architectural approach as sculptural, and the gallery certainly feels like a work of art. Each ceiling and wall has a different height and curve, and huge glass curtain walls refract the sunlight in unique ways, such that the building itself interplays with the world-class artwork it displays.

MAKING WAVES

The Guggenheim's impact far transcends architecture and art, however. Before it was commissioned by the Solomon R Guggenheim Foundation (which also funded Guggenheim museums in New York City and Venice), Bilbao was ignored by tourists and left stagnant after decades of industrial decline. The museum changed all that. Though its design was controversial with locals, it was an instant success among visitors and single-handedly put Bilbao on the tourist map, attracting millions of people each year; its impact was such that "the Bilbao effect" refers to a single attraction changing the fortunes of a whole city or area. Now that's a legacy.

📷
PHOTO OPPORTUNITY

The Guggenheim is striking from any angle, but climb up to the nearby La Salve Bridge for an elevated view. At sunset, light pools in the metal folds, and the whole building is reflected in the stillness of the Nervión river.

SINTRA · PORTUGAL

PENA PALACE

WHERE Estrada da Pena **TRANSPORT** Trains connect Sintra with Lisbon; the 434 bus runs from Sintra station to Pena Palace **INFORMATION** Open 9am–6pm daily (last entry: 5:30pm); ticket required (parquesdesintra.pt)

Only a flamboyant artist could have conceived Pena Palace, where technicolour turrets, domes and battlements rise from mist-wreathed mountains. You're in for a treat at this exuberant palace.

On a clear day, Pena Palace can be seen from Lisbon, and even by the standards of that photogenic city, it appears like a mirage – a fairytale castle erupting from the cork forests and hillsides of the horizon. Even when you get to Sintra, full to the brim with castles and fortresses, it's clear that Pena Palace is on another level. This is a jigsaw castle, with seemingly stuck-together sections each recalling a different era of history and corner of the planet, and painted in different palettes: bright yellow, coral red, purple and grey.

A DREAM COME TRUE

It's no surprise, given the palace's bright colours and bizarre construction, that its roots lie in the dreams of childhood. The site that became Pena Palace was once a crumbling monastery, reduced to ruins by a storm. The ruins enchanted the young Prince Ferdinand so much that, in the mid-19th century as King Ferdinand II of Portugal, he chose the site as a summer residence for the royal family.

Ferdinand's eye for the aesthetic earned him the title the "Artist King", and that nickname is well reflected in the eye-catching, layered design of Pena Palace. Its parapets, keeps and drawbridge evoke the days of medieval knights riding on horseback through forested mountains. Its onion domes and arches are Moorish Revival in style. The section at the castle's heart, meanwhile, is pure Manueline, the Portuguese late-Gothic style of ornamented stone balconies and blue-and-white azulejo ceramic tiles.

This exuberant mishmash of styles doesn't end at the exterior. Inside, the Smoking Room is crowned with a glorious ceiling, inlaid with swirling arabesques. The Stag Room recalls the hunting palaces of Germany, with antlered stag heads decorating the walls. Then there are the gardens, filled with groves and Classical statuary to resemble the grand villas of ancient Greece and Rome. Visiting Pena Palace is like taking a tour through the great castles of the world, all at once.

Right Colourful domes and turrets of the eclectic palace

Far right The Stag Room, where banquets were once held

MORE LIKE THIS

Portmeirion, UK
This highly unusual private Italianate village was eccentric architect Clough Williams-Ellis's childhood dream fulfilled when it was built in the 20th century. He took pieces of several demolished buildings and incorporated them into his own designs to create a fanciful bricolage of structures, which surround a central piazza.

Royal Pavilion, UK
Like an Indian palace squeezed through the prism of Regency England, this opulent seaside retreat, built for the Prince of Wales in 1823, is a riot of onion domes, cusped arches and sumptuous chandeliers.

Clockwise from top Canal houses in Grachtengordel; cycling around the city; Museum Van Loon's garden

14

AMSTERDAM · NETHERLANDS

AMSTERDAM CANAL DISTRICT

WHERE Grachtengordel features the best examples **TRANSPORT** Prinsengracht tram station is located in the heart of the area

Pretty can be practical – just look at Amsterdam's canalside houses. These elegant buildings can be found all over the city, but you'll find some of the best in the gorgeous district of Grachtengordel.

Amsterdam's canalside houses aren't your ordinary two-up, two-downs. They're skinny, tall, surprisingly deep and have roofs hidden behind decorative gables. Why? Because like much of the city, their distinctive design was dictated by their position on the water.

Pre-1585, the Dutch capital was confined within the Singel waterway, but over ensuing decades, four canals – the Prinsengracht, Keizersgracht and Herengracht, plus the Leidsegracht that connects them crossways – were created to help expand a city tight on living space. These canals formed a crescent-shaped district, the scenic Grachtengordel, which soon attracted wealthy families and merchants, who built their mansions on the edge of the water. All plots were the same size (hence the slim build and varying heights – if you can't build sideways, build up), but land lots did increase in size over the 17th century and some folks bought two plots to build even larger mansions.

That explains their shape, but what about their design? Amsterdam's canal houses are all topped by unique gables (decorative front apexes, usually hosting a small window), and some also feature hooks and cranes near the top of the building. These features were designed for hoisting belongings to upper-level rooms, rather than struggling up the houses' narrow, twisting staircases. Most have gardens, too. Hidden behind the tall façades, these leafy oases are the houses' best-kept secret (some open once a year as part of the city's beloved Open Garden Days).

Want to look inside? Many remain private apartments, but some of the buildings are open to the public as museums. For the grandest example, head to Museum Van Loon with its ornate interior symmetry and delightful formal gardens. Or you could simply stroll around the area, admiring the ingenuity of the Amsterdam architects who found a way to build by the water.

MUST-SEE BUILDINGS

WILLET-HOLTHUYSEN HOUSE
This double-mansion is decorated with 18th-century French-influenced furnishings and has a French-styled garden to match *(Herengracht 605)*.

BARTOLOTTI HOUSE
This grand, tangerine-hued building was at the time of its construction in 1620, probably the finest merchant's house on the canal front *(Herengracht 170)*.

MUSEUM VAN LOON
This 17th-century property, with its landscaped garden and historical furnishings, gives visitors an insight into the life of the canal houses' wealthy inhabitants, in this case the Van Loon family *(Keizersgracht 672)*.

GRACHTENMUSEUM
Housed in a 17th-century building, the Museum of the Canals takes visitors on a journey through Amsterdam's water-themed history *(Herengracht 386)*.

HOHENSCHWANGAU · GERMANY

NEUSCHWANSTEIN CASTLE

WHERE Neuschwansteinstraße 20 **TRANSPORT** Füssen is the nearest train station; buses run from here to the castle **INFORMATION** Open Apr–mid-Oct: 9am–6pm daily, mid-Oct–Mar: 10am–4pm daily; ticket required (neuschwanstein.de)

Though this fairytale castle in the clouds famously inspired Disney's *Sleeping Beauty*, nothing about it will leave you in a slumber. Born of an eccentric king's folly, Neuschwanstein is the ultimate passion project.

Glimpsing Neuschwanstein for the first time is utterly spellbinding. Perched on a rocky outcrop above the tiny hamlet of Hohenschwangau, and set high above the lakes of Forggensee, Alpsee and Schwansee, its towering façade defies logic.

This zany castle was the brainchild of King Ludwig II of Bavaria, a notoriously shy and enigmatic ruler who preferred fairytales and plays to royal duties. With a desire to retreat from public life in Munich (and put his creativity to good use), Ludwig commissioned Neuschwanstein in 1869. Construction, however, was beset with financial problems, and the Bavarian king even made concessions to Otto von Bismarck's Prussian government to secure secret funding. He intended to complete the castle in three years, but when he mysteriously died in 1886, it was still unfinished – and remains so today.

AN ENDURING VISION

A few weeks after Ludwig's death, the castle was opened to the public (anything to help pay off his debts). It's been a hit ever since: more than 60 million people have visited, and 1.5 million come to snoop around on a guided tour every year.

As soon as you cross Neuschwanstein's drawbridge, the scale of Ludwig's vision is clear; the castle's fanciful turrets pierce the clouds. Inside, everything is imbued with Ludwig's vivid imagination. A gravity-defying chandelier dominates the Byzantine-styled Throne Hall (which was never fitted with a throne), while walls swirl with colour in the Singer's Hall, where rich murals and gold leaf drip down from a panelled ceiling onto a parquet floor. The castle might stand as a cautionary tale against hubris, but it also represents one man's fanatical quest for beauty. In that, he certainly succeeded.

Right The castle, set in magnificent mountain scenery

Far right The Singer's Hall

PHOTO OPPORTUNITY

To get the quintessential shot of Neuschwanstein, head to the iron Marienbrücke (Mary's Bridge) in Schwangau. From here, you'll get a panorama of the castle with the rolling farmland and Forggensee beyond.

The striking Elbphilharmonie, with its 600 curved window panels

HAMBURG · GERMANY

ELBPHILHARMONIE

WHERE Platz der Deutschen Einheit 4 **TRANSPORT** Baumwall is the nearest station (on the U3 underground train line) **INFORMATION** The free-to-visit Plaza is open 10am–midnight daily; check online for performance schedule (elbphilharmonie.de)

Is it a sea monster risen from the deep? A vast ocean liner? Maybe a giant iceberg? No one quite agrees what Hamburg's crystalline Elbphilharmonie most resembles, but few doubt that it's one of the world's most staggering concert halls.

When Swiss architects Herzog & de Meuron proposed to build a grand concert hall in a disused 1960s brick warehouse at the western tip of Hamburg's old harbour, they were faced with a problem. How could this awkwardly narrow building, with limited foundations, encompass a 2,000-seat, state-of-the-art auditorium? The solution was simple brilliance. They built upwards, placing a shimmering glass box on the old brick base, and suspending the grand hall from the roof like a giant cocoon. Topped off with a soaring, wave-like roofline that recalls the rippling surface of the flowing Elbe river below, the concert hall has fast become the modern emblem of Germany's boomtown port city.

A HALL FOR ALL

Costing an eye-watering €866 million, the Elbphilharmonie may be the world's most expensive concert hall, yet it's refreshingly open to all comers. Anticipation builds as you ride Europe's longest curved escalator to the Plaza, the public observation deck sandwiched between the two massive structures. Once inside, you're greeted by a gorgeous, light-filled space, where nothing distracts from the huge windows that frame the horizon on either side. Step out, coffee (or something stronger) in hand, onto the wraparound terrace to survey the panorama and raise a toast in celebration. This modern marvel may have cost the earth, but sometimes only the best will do.

WHEN TO GO

Book a tour through the website (offered several times a week, but times vary depending on the concert schedule) to explore the superb centrepiece, the Grand Hall. From the waterfall-like organ to the cell-like "skin" walls, fashioned for perfect acoustics, it's a beautiful, organic space.

DESSAU-ROSSLAU • GERMANY

BAUHAUS DESSAU

WHERE Gropiusallee 38 **TRANSPORT** Dessau Hauptbahnhof is the nearest station (trains to Berlin) **INFORMATION** Open Apr–Oct: 10am–6pm Tue–Sun (Nov–Feb: to 5pm) (bauhaus-dessau.de)

Function first, form second: that was the Bauhaus USP. And where better to see examples of this innovative 20th-century movement than at its old art school, Bauhaus Dessau?

Bauhaus broke the mould. Gone were the frills and fancy façades of earlier architecture movements; in their place came functional designs, clean lines and an emphasis on mass production. This avant-garde movement originated in Weimar, Germany in 1919 and subsequently set up schools in Dessau and Berlin. It was highly influential, and today you'll find examples all over the world – most famously in the White City area of Tel Aviv, home to some 4,000 Bauhaus buildings. Fittingly, however, the Bauhaus art school in Dessau is the movement's standard-bearer.

Designed by Bauhaus founder Walter Gropius and completed in 1926, the school showcases all the characteristics of the movement: it's highly functional, lacking in ornamentation and largely horizontal. Its interconnected wings all feature flat roofs (designed to be walkable), and one building also hosts a huge glass curtain to allow natural light to fill the classrooms. As in all Bauhaus schools, classes here were taught in workshop settings and covered all manner of art (from furniture design to arts and crafts).

Incredibly, given its outsized impact on design, the Bauhaus movement lasted just 14 years. In 1933, the Nazis (having won elections in Dessau) branded the art school "cultural Bolshevism" and forced its closure. The building itself wasn't destroyed, however (it's now a museum), and architects continued to be inspired by the "less is more" approach – just look at the world's Brutalist buildings.

Right Bauhaus-designed buildings in the Dessau school complex

WHEN TO GO

The complex hosts numerous events over the year (including art exhibits and craft workshops), so be sure to check its online calendar. Visitors can even stay overnight in one of the complex's restored studio rooms.

WARSAW · POLAND

PALACE OF CULTURE AND SCIENCE

WHERE Plac Defilad 1 **TRANSPORT** Center (metro), Warsaw Central (train) **INFORMATION** Open 10am–8pm daily; tickets are required for the observation deck (pkin.pl)

Nicknamed "the elephant in lacy underwear" for its size and ornate style, the Stalinist Palace of Culture and Science isn't quite what you'd expect to see in downtown Warsaw.

The world's best buildings have a story to tell – and nothing about the story of this building is predictable. Bequeathed to Warsaw as a gift by Soviet dictator Joseph Stalin in 1952, the Palace of Culture and Science was designed in the Stalinist style to resemble the Seven Sisters skyscrapers in Moscow. It took 40 million bricks and 3,500 Soviet workers to complete the Tetris-like group of five stacked towers, with garishly spiky parapets and sumptuous interiors (picture heavy glass chandeliers and marble columns).

Its great bulk and perceived overblown style meant it stuck out like a sore thumb in Warsaw's low-rise downtown, quickly earning it a slew of fondly disparaging nicknames. Polish poet Władysław Broniewski called it "the nightmare dream of a drunken pastry chef", and it was often known as "Stalin's birthday cake". It still provokes extreme reactions today, with some calling for its destruction (it remains a brooding symbol of Soviet domination). But it's not all bad. In 1967, the Rolling Stones played in the palace's concert hall – the first gig by a Western band behind the Iron Curtain, and an event that paved the way for the building's modern use as a music venue. There's a cinema, observation deck and two museums here, too.

Next page Warsaw's massive Palace of Culture and Science

The oval-shaped Colosseum, an icon of ancient Rome

ROME • ITALY

COLOSSEUM

WHERE Piazza del Colosseo, 1 **TRANSPORT** Colosseo (metro, bus) is the nearest station **INFORMATION** Open Apr–Sep: 8:30am–7:15pm daily; Oct: 8:30am–6:30pm daily; Nov–Feb: 8:30am–4:30pm daily; ticket required; free for under 18s (colosseo.it)

As far as ancient sights go, the Colosseum might well be the most impressive. Once the setting for gruesome gladiator fights, this epic venue is no longer famed for its bloody combat, but for the spectacle of the building itself.

Its name means "colossal", and the first thing that strikes you about Rome's Colosseum is indeed its sheer size – this was the largest amphitheatre in the ancient world, and in its 1st-century CE heyday, it could seat up to 80,000 spectators. The venue's epic scale befitted the high drama of the events that were held here: gladiatorial duels, hunts of exotic animals like tigers and rhinoceroses, and the condemnation of criminals to the lions' den.

While the nature of popular entertainment may have changed since the Romans ruled, in some ways, events at the Colosseum were not so different from modern-day sporting events. Stalls outside sold food – olives, hazelnuts and even pizza-like flatbreads called *pinsa* – and spectators streamed in through 80 arched gates, many of which are still standing today. The gates were numbered to make entry more efficient, and they led into wide concourses for easier flow of the crowd; when events were over, passages called *vomitoria* allowed spectators to exit quickly. All of this helped make the Colosseum so special – far from being just a grand show of wealth for powerful patrons, the building put the punters' experience first. Its construction was also ahead of its time: light, strong travertine (limestone) from the quarries of Tivoli was used to build the outer wall, which in part explains why it's still standing after two millennia.

HYPE FOR THE HYPOGEUM

The Colosseum pushed the boat out when it came to the technology of stagecraft, too. Early in its existence, the Colosseum's arena floor was flooded via an aqueduct, so that it could be used for mock naval battles. Later, during the reign of Domitian (r 81–96 CE), the naval battles and flooding system were abandoned and the floor was remodelled to incorporate

Right The exposed tunnels of the hypogeum

Far right Grand gateways, now in ruins

a hypogeum – an elaborate underground warren of tunnels and cages where gladiators, animals and pieces of set decoration were concealed beneath the stage floor. Trapdoors covered with sand on the arena floor and systems of pulleys connected the hypogeum with the arena so that characters could spring up into the action, as if from nowhere; a magical piece of theatrical trickery, which only added to the already heightened drama.

FROM PLEBS TO PRIESTESSES

The people loved the drama. Folks flooded in for events, which were happily free (paid for by the emperor or by wealthy individuals out of a sense of public duty and as a means of consolidating power and popularity with the public). Yet despite no money changing hands, ticketing at the Colosseum was far from egalitarian. The premier seats were in the lower tier, closest to the action. Cream of the crop, with the best views and cushioned seats, were the boxes at either end of the stadium; the north box was reserved for the emperor and his entourage, and the south box for the Vestal Virgins, Rome's highest priestesses. Arrayed around them were senators, other nobility and the property-owning equestrian class. Plebeians (ordinary citizens) occupied the next tier, while women and enslaved people were only allowed into the highest tier, which had the worst views and was usually standing only.

You'll get a much better view today. Visitors can walk amid the intricate cells and tunnels of the hypogeum (the arena floor has gone) and climb the steep steps between the first and second tiers of seating. As for performances, well, you'll merely be watching other tourists – gladiators only fight on the big screen these days.

PHOTO OPPORTUNITY

For an atmospheric, time-worn perspective on the Colosseum, take a picture from the Via Celio Vibenna on the monument's southeastern side. The arches on this side are riddled with holes, a legacy of the Middle Ages, when the metal clamps in the stonework were looted to make weapons.

+ WHILE YOU'RE HERE

Want to tick off all the ancient sites in the Eternal City? You'll need a while. Akin to a living museum, the Italian capital is rife with ancient sites, so, start with the big-hitters. Second only to the Colosseum is the Forum, once the hub of daily life. This civic space once hosted processions, elections and criminal trials. Today, there are still traces of many ancient structures, including the Arch of Septimius Severus and the Temple of Saturn. Nearby, you'll also find the Baths of Caracalla, one of the largest bathhouses in the ancient world (the Romans were a bit obsessed with personal hygiene). They're well preserved, too, complete with the ingenious underfloor water-heating systems. And then there's Palatine Hill. Often considered the birthplace of Rome, this area still contains the ruins of the Palace of Domitian, the House of Tiberius and various other ancient monuments.

Top *The Classical columned entrance to the Pantheon*

Below *Light flooding through the famous oculus*

ROME · ITALY

PANTHEON

WHERE Piazza della Rotonda **TRANSPORT** Barberini (metro) is the nearest station **INFORMATION** Open 9am–7pm daily (last entry: 6:30pm); ticket required (portale.museiitaliani.it)

Rome is home to countless ancient ruins, but none are as well preserved as the Pantheon. Dedicated to "all the gods" and famed for its domed interior and central oculus, this stately Roman temple is an architectural marvel.

From the outside, the Pantheon appears deceptively simple and quasi austere. Its portico is lined with 16 Corinthian columns, behind which lies a vast, seemingly plain drum. Step inside, though, and you'll realize that looks can be deceiving. The building's interior is a perfectly solved maths puzzle: the towering dome has a diameter equal to the exact height of the building. The dome itself is a veritable feat of engineering, too – it's the world's largest unreinforced concrete dome, its weight distributed on thick surrounding walls and eight pylons. Think that's awe-inspiring? Consider how old the building is: originally constructed in 27 BCE by statesman Marcus Agrippa, the temple was rebuilt by Emperor Hadrian, way back in 125 CE.

EYE TO THE SKY

The building's perfect hemispherical geometry isn't the only architectural marvel here. Perhaps the Pantheon's most famous feature is its 9-m (30-ft)-wide oculus. This opening at the very centre of the dome is akin to a cosmic eye, connecting worshippers to the gods above. Prayers can rise unencumbered, but the heavens can open too (to many visitors' surprise, rain falls freely through the oculus). The Romans were well prepared, however: ingenious engineers constructed a nifty drainage system to prevent any flooding.

But really, the oculus is all about light. The opening works like a sundial, with rays moving along the walls and marking the passage of time. Phenomena occur throughout the year, too: during the summer solstice, sunlight projects a giant shining disc on the floor, while at noon on the 21 April (the founding date of Rome) light streams through the oculus and perfectly illuminates the Pantheon's entrance. There's science behind it, but this interplay between light and architecture does feel a bit like magic. Perhaps the gods really are gazing through the oculus after all.

MORE LIKE THIS

The cupola of the Cathedral of Santa Maria del Fiore, Italy
Famed Italian architect Filippo Brunelleschi meticulously studied the Pantheon's dome before he began constructing Florence's most iconic landmark. Made of brick instead of concrete, Brunelleschi's octagonal dome is, to this day, the largest masonry dome ever built.

VENICE · ITALY

ST MARK'S BASILICA

WHERE Piazza San Marco 328 **TRANSPORT** San Zaccaria (vaporetto) is the nearest station **INFORMATION** Open 9:30am–5:15pm daily (from 2pm Sunday; last admission 4:45pm); ticket required (basilicasanmarco.it)

Visitors get giddy in Piazza San Marco. This central Venetian square is packed with gorgeous buildings – including the soaring Campanile and the elegant Palazzo Ducale – but none can compete with the dazzling St Mark's Basilica.

Whether they're winding through little alleyways or floating down quaint canals, tourists usually have one destination in mind when visiting Venice: St Mark's Square. Long the bustling hub of the city, this vast Venetian piazza is lined with magnificent buildings, peppered with pavement cafés and overlooked by the lofty Campanile. As your eyes rove the surroundings, absorbing the ostentatious façades and bustling crowds, they'll inevitably snag on the square's most spectacular resident: Basilica di San Marco.

It's a testament to St Mark's Basilica's beauty that it stands out among such fierce competition. Crowned with five huge domes, this Byzantine extravaganza is embellished with golden mosaics, graceful icons and ornate marble carvings. It was consecrated in 1094, taking centuries to build and overseen by numerous Venetian doges (dukes). None of them held back. Treasures came from overseas empires – including bronze horse sculptures from Constantinople – and new decorative elements were added nearly every century. For a long while, the building acted as the doges' private chapel, but in 1807, it became the cathedral for the city – a fittingly grand one for a place as dazzling as Venice.

St Mark's Basilica is equally magnificent inside. Enter through its grand portals and you'll immediately be struck by its mosaics, which carpet the entirety of the Basilica's walls, vaults and domes and shimmer in the light that filters through. Most date to the mid-13th century, though several were developed over the course of some eight centuries.

PRECIOUS JEWELS

As prized as the mosaics are, they're not the Basilica's most precious work. That honour goes to the Pala d'Oro, a stunning golden altar panel housed in the Sanctuary. Commissioned in 976 in Constantinople, it was enriched over the years by various Byzantines and Venetians. The final result? A panel adorned with a staggering number of precious stones and gems, including 300 sapphires, 300 emeralds, 400 garnets and 1,300 pearls. It's considered to be the world's most valuable Byzantine altarpiece, and seeing it is worth the admission to the Basilica alone.

St Mark's Basilica's ornate exterior

The Duomo's enormous dome towering over Florence's skyline

FLORENCE · ITALY

RENAISSANCE FLORENCE

WHERE Throughout the city **TRANSPORT** Sights are walkable from Santa Maria Novella railway station

It's easy to forget not only the day but the decade in Florence, a living museum that holds the title of the birthplace of the Renaissance. This is the place to go misty-eyed over palazzos, basilicas and duomos.

The concept of a revival, or Renaissance, came about in the 14th century when a group of Florentine artists sought to break with the conventions of the Middle Ages by reviving the literature, art and learnings of Classical antiquity. This awakening to the grandeur of ancient Greece and Rome created a new form of art and architecture, and nowhere was it more pronounced than in Florence.

FAMILY FORTUNES
Ideas were one thing, but turning them into reality required the kind of wealth that the Medici family had in spades. Rulers of Florence and patrons of the arts, they commissioned and financed groundbreaking new buildings, supporting architects who would go on to become the Renaissance's most prominent players, like Filippo Brunelleschi and Michelozzo. As well as financing public structures, the Medici wanted a personal piece of the action, which is why many of the finest Renaissance buildings were their own private residences. Take the Palazzo Medici Riccardi, the home of Cosimo de' Medici, or Palazzo Pitti, a ducal residence, home to the expansive Boboli Gardens. These homes bear the hallmarks of Renaissance architecture with their arcaded courtyards, harmonious Classical proportions and spectacular frescoes and sculptures, courtesy of artists like Donatello and Leonardo da Vinci.

AN IMPRESSIVE DOME
As well as private residences and palaces, religious and secular buildings, as well as bridges and squares, got the Renaissance treatment. Architects started to embrace both epic grandeur and elegant harmony; the fashion called for columns, rich decoration, pedimented windows, cornices and extravagant domes, the latter of which you'll

Clockwise from left
The courtyard of the Palazzo Medici Riccardi; Basilica di Santa Maria Novella; the Piazzale degli Uffizi, with the Uffizi galleries on either side

see no matter where you are in the city. Yes, we're talking about the apogee of Renaissance architecture: the dome of the Duomo di Firenze.

Construction of the cathedral started in 1296, but by the time the Renaissance was in full swing, it was missing its key piece: the dome. It was a challenge for all those who attempted to build it, and so in 1418, a competition sought those who could provide a solution. The winner? Brunelleschi, who proposed an ingenious self-supporting dome design, combining his knowledge of Gothic vaulting traditions with Classical architecture.

Brunelleschi travelled to Rome to study ancient Roman buildings and architectural features – columns, pediments, pillars, arches – to create a harmonious design that came to symbolize a new era in architecture. With an external diameter of 55 m (180 ft), the octagonal dome is made of stone and brick, with an inner shell that provides a platform to support the outer shell. Completed in 1436, it's the largest masonry vault ever built, and was the first true masterpiece of Renaissance architecture.

RENAISSANCE FOREVER

It's 463 steps to reach the top of the dome, from where unobstructed views look out over the city's Renaissance core and a whole host of Florence's most significant sights. One such example is the Basilica di Santa Maria Novella to the west, its white-and-green marble façade glistening in the sun. But it's not just about what's on the outside of these buildings. Within them all are plenty of Renaissance treasures, the best of which lie inside the world-famous Uffizi and Accademia galleries, home to seminal works by Donatello, da Vinci, Michelangelo and Sandro Botticelli, to name a few. You can't help but think they'd be proud to see how little their city has changed since they left their mark.

PHOTO OPPORTUNITY

Make for Piazzale Michelangelo on the south bank of the River Arno to take in the city skyline, with the Duomo rising to the northwest. Aim for sunset, when the sun paints the city in a riot of pinks and reds.

MUST-SEE BUILDINGS

PALAZZO VECCHIO
This palazzo has retained its medieval appearance, but much of the interior was remodelled for Duke Cosimo I in 1540 *(Piazza della Signoria)*.

PALAZZO MEDICI RICCARDI
The city's first great Renaissance palazzo was built to an austere design by Michelozzo for Cosimo il Vecchio, and was home to the Medici for 100 years *(Via Camillo Cavour, 3)*.

DUOMO AND BAPTISTRY
Florence Cathedral's orange-tiled dome is the city's most famous symbol, but don't overlook the baptistry: its doors are a pivotal work of Renaissance sculpture *(Piazza del Duomo)*.

THE UFFIZI
Florence's iconic gallery, built between 1560 and 1580, doesn't just hold Renaissance masterpieces: it is one. Architect Vasari used iron reinforcement to create an almost continuous wall of glass on the upper storey *(Piazzale degli Uffizi, 6)*.

EUROPE

ROME · ITALY

ST PETER'S

WHERE Piazza San Pietro, Vatican City **TRANSPORT** Ottaviano-San Pietro (metro) is the nearest station **INFORMATION** Opening hours vary by season, check website (basilicasanpietro.va); there's a fee to climb the dome

Could this be the most famous church in the world? The spiritual centre of the Catholic Church, the great basilica of St Peter's draws pilgrims from all over the world for all manner of reasons.

Clockwise from above St Peter's, which took more than 100 years to build, completed in 1626; walking through the colonnade of St Peter's Square; the basilica's ornate ceiling

Vatican City, the world capital of Catholicism, is the world's smallest state, but it packs a heck of a lot into its 43 ha (106 acres), most notably its famous centrepiece: St Peter's. This basilica was built on the site where St Peter – the founding leader of the Church – was martyred and buried in 61 CE. Just as famous is the piazza it stands on, St Peter's Square, which is always packed with pilgrims when the Pope is due to appear (and even when he isn't).

A MASS BUILDING

The first thing you notice is the size. This is, after all, one of the largest churches in the world, and the 187-m- (614-ft-) long, marble-encrusted interior contains 11 chapels and 45 altars. That's a lot of space to show off some incredible art, which some of the world's most important artists of the 16th and 17th centuries happily provided. Take Michelangelo's *Pietà*, on display immediately beyond the entrance. Carved from a solid block of Carrara marble, the sculpture depicts the Virgin Mary holding a lifeless Christ. It was Michelangelo, too, who designed the basilica's towering dome, although it was only built up to the drum during his lifetime. The world's tallest dome, it's a beautiful piece of work, with mosaic tiers above the drum portraying the busts of the 16 popes who are buried in the basilica.

One of the best ways to take in the church's scale is from the gallery, the interior balcony you reach when climbing the dome. From here, you can admire Bernini's colossal 28-m (92-ft) gilded bronze *baldacchino* (canopy), which fits comfortably over the altar, its twisted Baroque columns towering above the human frame and marking the location of St Peter's tomb below. If you can tear yourself away from the basilica, make the Vatican Museums your next stop, where more riches await – Sistine Chapel, anyone?

MORE LIKE THIS

St Paul's Cathedral, UK
With a dome arguably as famous as St Peter's, this spectacular cathedral by Christopher Wren is an unmistakable feature of London's skyline. Its innovative design consists of three nested domes: a hemispherical outer dome, an inner dome and a hidden brick cone.

Church of Saint Sava, Serbia
With its astonishing size, cross-shaped floorplan and commanding dome, the principal cathedral of the Serbian Orthodox Church is a masterpiece of religious architecture. The cupola, the inner vault of the dome, is home to a magnificent mosaic.

Milan's Duomo, a marvel in marble

MILAN · ITALY

MILAN'S DUOMO

WHERE Piazza del Duomo **TRANSPORT** The Duomo (metro) is the nearest station
INFORMATION Open 9am–7pm (last entry: 6pm); in summer, the terraces (on the roof) are open until 8pm; ticket required (ticket.duomomilano.it)

Italy isn't short of cathedrals, but this might be its most extravagant. Milan's Gothic-style Duomo went a little wild when it came to ornamentation: spot the gangs of gargoyles, lofty spires and over 3,400 intricately adorned statues.

It'll come as no surprise to hear that Milan's Duomo didn't go up in a day. This extravagant cathedral – one of the largest churches in the world – took nearly six centuries (and who knows how much money) to complete. The initial foundations were laid in 1386 under the first Duke of Milan, Gian Galeazzo Visconti, who sought to construct a building that would rival France and Germany's great Gothic cathedrals. But instead of using traditional brick, he chose to use marble for its construction – the rosy-hued stone was extracted from Candoglia near Lake Maggiore and transported to the centre of Milan along the city's canals. Sculptors, architects, engineers and glaziers were called in from all over Europe, and workshops opened in Milan to supply the large stained-glass windows. Bit by bit, century by century, the cathedral began to take shape. But it didn't stay Gothic forever. During the 16th century, Renaissance ruled and many elements in the cathedral were cast in this style – the wooden choir stalls, the presbytery and the baptistery. Work then slowed in the 1600s, as attention shifted towards minor details and the façade work, and the cathedral wasn't actually completed until 1965 (when the last portal was installed).

There's beauty in every aspect, but the statues that cover the façade are the highlight. Look out for Neo-Classical sculptor Camillo Pacetti's *The New Law*, said to have inspired Frédéric Auguste Bartholdi's Statue of Liberty in New York. And don't miss the *Madonnina*, a Gothic gilded bronze statue of the Virgin Mary that was placed on the central spire in 1774 – it's the undisputed symbol of Milan. But for the best views, you'll need to go high. The Duomo's roof is open to visitors, giving you a chance to gaze at its 135 spires up close and walk atop layer upon layer of history – a whole six centuries of architectural development.

PISA · ITALY

LEANING TOWER OF PISA

WHERE Piazza del Duomo **TRANSPORT** Torre 1 is the closest bus stop **INFORMATION** Opening hours vary, check website (opapisa.it); buy tickets to climb the tower

Should you lean against it? Push it over? Perch it on top of an ice cream cone? The photo opportunities afforded by Europe's most amusing building never get boring.

There's hardly a more popular photo opportunity in Europe than the chance to play with perspective at the Leaning Tower of Pisa. But was the infamous tilt, which draws in millions of tourists every year, an intentional part of the design? Not one bit. The lean is actually a result of the building's unstable foundations, but it's become so iconic that the Italian authorities have resisted repairing it beyond ensuring it won't *actually* topple over.

This decision would have seemed ironic to the tower's early builders, who were likely tearing their hair out over its unique challenges. Construction began in 1173 and took 199 years to finish, partly because the tower had started to lean over just five years into its construction, with a succession of engineers hired to remedy it. The identity of that first architect remains a mystery (perhaps nobody wanted to be associated with a wonky tower), but experts have deduced that it may have been a local architect, Diotisalvi.

Whoever designed it should be proud, though. This is a building of exquisite artistry, built from marble as white as ivory and carved into eight arcades of colonnaded arches that reach to more than 56 m (184 ft) high. The adjacent Duomo and Baptistery bear a similar style, and together make up one of the most beautiful architectural complexes in Italy, so do be sure to explore – once you've taken those obligatory perspective-bending photos, of course.

Right The famous tower, with a 4° tilt

BRAN · ROMANIA

BRAN CASTLE

WHERE Strada General Traian Moșoiu 24 **TRANSPORT** Brasov is the nearest train station; you can catch a bus from here to the castle **INFORMATION** Opening hours vary, check website (bran-castle.com); ticket required

Known as the home of Count Dracula, Bran Castle actually has nothing to do with the legendary vampire – but that does little to diminish its drama. Perched on a rocky outcrop amid mountain forests, this is a building to sink your teeth into.

Standing lonely on a high forested pass in the Carpathian Mountains, Bran Castle would make a fine dwelling for a blood-sucking Transylvanian aristocrat. But its alternative moniker of "Dracula's Castle" is little more than a marketing gimmick. Yes, the namesake vampire of Bram Stoker's novel lives out his days in a Romanian castle perched high above a valley, eerily similar to this one, but Bran Castle has no documented connection to either Stoker or Vlad "the Impaler" Dracula, who inspired the character. In fact, its most famous real-life occupant was Marie, the last queen of Romania.

A GOTHIC HOME

Its lack of association with a sharp-toothed vampire doesn't make the castle any less Gothic. Bran Castle is all about drama: a collection of turrets and towers clustered on a rocky precipice, with white-stone half-timbered walls reaching up to terracotta-tiled roofs. A steep staircase leads to the main double doors, beyond which you'll find many classic creepy castle features: a dingy secret passageway, weapons hung on walls and a bearskin rug in the music room, not to mention views out over thickly tree-clad slopes.

All that said, the place feels less imposing and, dare we say, more homely than it appears from the outside. Take Queen Marie's apartment, with its modest bed and dark-wood furniture. The immortal Dracula may not have a link to Bran Castle, but this would certainly be a fine place to spend eternity.

WHEN TO GO

Still convinced Dracula's lurking here? Visit on the closest Saturday to Halloween to attend a spooky party, when the castle is filled with ghoulish decorations, actors and audio-visual displays.

Next page The moody castle, built in the 14th century

Clockwise from left The sunlit Parthenon, the jewel atop the Acropolis's crown; statues decorating the façade; the near-identical Doric columns

ATHENS · GREECE

PARTHENON

WHERE Athens 105 58 **TRANSPORT** Acropoli (metro) and Erechtheion (bus) are the nearest stations **INFORMATION** Open Apr–Sep: 8am–7:30pm daily; Oct–Mar: 8am–5pm daily; ticket required (theacropolismuseum.gr)

Is there a more evocative symbol of the Classical age than this? Looming over the city of Athens, the spectacular Parthenon is the most perfect ancient Greek temple still in existence.

It's impossible to ignore the Parthenon. Wherever you go in Athens, your eyes can't help but gaze up at this ancient temple, sat atop a rugged hill overlooking the city. It's been there since the birth of Western civilization, and despite centuries of earthquakes, sieges and invasions, it still stands strong today. Remarkably strong, in fact – for a temple that's nearly 2,500 years old.

But let's rewind. The Parthenon was built way back in the 5th century BCE as a temple to the Greek goddess Athena. It soon became the most famous structure atop the Acropolis – a hilltop citadel that acted as the religious and cultural centre of Athens and is still home to a number of other ruined temples and sanctuaries. Ancient Greeks flocked here to pay their respects, and today the site still involves a pilgrimage of sorts: an uphill, half-hour walk leads you along a path of flagstones, polished smooth by millions of footsteps before you, and up to the top of the hill.

A TRIP BACK IN TIME

Seeing the Parthenon from afar is dazzling (particularly at sunrise or sunset, when it glows in the Grecian sun), but seeing it up close is even better. History swirls around this atmospheric site: walk beside its Doric columns, which rise amid a field of marble rubble and half-broken statues, and you'll be whisked back to the days of Socrates (thought to have helped build the Acropolis); or gaze at its intricate carvings, which depict stories like the Trojan War, and you'll hear the cries of warriors and clash of swords. It's easy to get swept up, but be sure to take a step back to survey the building in its entirety. With 46 identical columns, it looks perfect, doesn't it? Turns out, they're not identical. The Parthenon has few straight lines and uses the technique of "optical refinement", with slight curves and irregular column spacings compensating for the curvature of the human eye. It's an illusion of symmetry, a portrait of perfect imperfection.

PHOTO OPPORTUNITY

Walk to the top of Lycabettus Hill, the highest vantage point in Athens, for the best sunset views over the Acropolis, with the glittering Aegean Sea beyond. The summit is a 20-minute walk from Syntagma Square in the centre of Athens.

Right The multiple domes and minarets of Hagia Sophia

Below The mosque's ornately decorated nave

ISTANBUL · TURKEY

HAGIA SOPHIA

WHERE Ayasofya Meydanı 1 **TRANSPORT** Eminönü ferry terminal or Sultanahmet (tram) are the nearest stations **INFORMATION** Open 9am–7:30pm daily; tickets can be purchased from the booth by the Fountain of Sultan Ahmet III

The epitome of Byzantine architecture, this massive mosque has been in situ for over 1,600 years. It's nestled on a hillside at the confluence where east meets west, and its miraculous architecture blends two worlds and two religions.

Straddling the continents of Asia and Europe, Istanbul has long been a crossroads of cultures. It was founded back in 657 BCE, and since then it's worn many names (most famously, Constantinople), been the capital of great empires (Roman, Byzantine and Ottoman) and acted as a hub of multiple religions. Today, its blended history is still clear to see, most notably in its legendary landmark: Hagia Sophia.

It's hard to comprehend the size of Istanbul's iconic mosque from the outside (your neck can only bend so far back to see its ashen domes and slender minarets), so head inside instead. Here, the mosque's cavernous nave yawns above you, with giant medallions (displaying Quranic verses written in golden calligraphy) on its walls, huge chandeliers hanging from the decorative ceiling and a plush carpet blanketing its floor. The most striking feature, however, is the dome. This epic rounded roof is a whopping 31 m (101 ft) in diameter, lined with 40 arched windows and decorated with beautiful mosaics.

STANDING STRONG

Hagia Sophia wasn't always a mosque. Initially, from 360 CE, the site served as Constantinople's Eastern Orthodox cathedral, with the then Byzantine emperor, Justinian I, overseeing the roof's construction during the 6th century. Upon completion in 537 CE, it became the first fully pendentive dome in existence. After collapsing in 558 CE, it was rebuilt even bigger, balanced on a square base to transfer its enormous weight. Since then, it's withstood successive earthquakes, a testament to its revolutionary engineering.

After the Fall of Constantinople in 1453, the cathedral was converted into a mosque, which, bar an 85-year spell as a museum, it remains today. The building's minarets are a clear example of this transformation, although traces of its Christian heritage still linger – spot the mosaic in the southwest vestibule depicting the Virgin Mary cradling the infant Jesus. The idea of shared space permeates the building, something Istanbul knows a thing or two about.

+ **WHILE YOU'RE HERE**

You'll find another important religious site a stone's throw from Hagia Sophia: Sultan Ahmed Mosque. Finished in 1617, this Ottoman architectural highlight is more commonly known as the Blue Mosque, owing to the 20,000-plus hand-painted Iznik tiles (ceramics from the eponymous Turkish town) decorating its blue-tinted interior. The building also features a central dome and four semi-domes over its prayer hall, plus six minarets.

29

GRAZ · AUSTRIA

KUNSTHAUS GRAZ

WHERE Lendkai 1 **TRANSPORT** Trams run to Südtiroler Platz/Kunsthaus **INFORMATION** Open 10am–6pm Tue–Sun; ticket required (museum-joanneum.at/en/kunsthaus-graz)

Built to be a talking point, Graz's "friendly alien" is the city's ultimate drawcard, the face of endless tourism brochures and even a postage stamp.

Neighbouring centuries-old Habsburg-dynasty architecture, Kunsthaus Graz feels like an imposter on Graz's red-roofed skyline, a huge alien that's landed on the wrong planet. The art museum was built in 2003, the same year that Graz was awarded the European Capital of Culture, and the outlandish design was deliberate – bold enough to signal Graz's cultural prowess, revitalize an overlooked part of the city and do good for the economy.

The extraterrestrial-like tentacles that protrude from its blue roof are a hallmark of "blobitecture", a late 20th-century and early noughties phenomenon where architecture forsook straight, solid lines and embraced the amorphous. Perhaps even more unusual, however, is that the design incorporates a 19th-century building: the Eisernes Haus, or Iron House. Once a department store and café, the Iron House fell into neglect following structural problems, only to be restored and linked with Kunsthaus Graz in 2003 – a brilliant way to bridge the old with the new. You'll end up visiting both; start in the Iron House, which serves as the museum's foyer, then ascend into the alien via a "travelator", an escalator that slowly travels to the exhibition areas. This clever design achieves exactly what it set out to do: regenerate a lesser-visited part of the city by attracting new businesses nearby and drawing people from all over the world. That's a friendly alien, indeed.

Right The marrow-shaped building; the contemporary art inside

PHOTO OPPORTUNITY

Take your camera out at night, when the building becomes a light sculpture thanks to the BIX (Big Pixels) façade: a sheet of 930 fluorescent lights with adjustable brightness, on which lights can be switched on or off to make giant-sized pictures and words.

 30

COPENHAGEN · DENMARK

AMAGER BAKKE

WHERE Vindmøllevej 6 **TRANSPORT** Take the bus to the Amager Bakke stop **INFORMATION** Open 11am–7pm daily (to 5pm Sun) (copenhill.dk)

How do you get people excited about a power plant? Top it with a ski slope and give it the Danish design treatment, of course.

It's no exaggeration to call this one of the most ingenious municipal environmental initiatives in history. Amager Bakke, or CopenHill as it's known, opened in 2017, contributing to Copenhagen's mission to become the world's first carbon-neutral city. But this power plant isn't a one-trick pony. As well as converting the waste of 500,000 residents to produce heat and electricity for 150,000, it's also the ultimate outdoor playground.

CITY GOALS

Comprised of aluminium blocks, Amager Bakke resembles a giant ramp. It's 85 m (280 ft) high at the upper end, and the roof (topped with grass, by the way) slants at gradients of up to 35 per cent, forming the capital's steepest hill. The clincher? It's sturdy enough to support a ski and sledding area. The 400-m- (1,312-ft-) long piste, made by Italian dry ski slope manufacturers Neveplast, offers the only opportunity to try year-round skiing and mountain running in pancake-flat Copenhagen. Besides a ski slope, there's also a slice of parkland for walking, running and taking in the views.

Rather than treating a power plant as a monstrosity not worthy of attention, Amager Bakke shows that such buildings can be wondrously woven into a city's fabric, and even be beneficial to its citizens. How often can you say you've skied down a power plant? Pretty cool if you ask us.

Next page The urban mountain bringing height to Copenhagen

EUROPE

Clockwise from left The Hungarian Geological Institute; an ornate lift in the Postal Savings Bank; the bank's exterior

BUDAPEST · HUNGARY

BUDAPEST ART NOUVEAU

WHERE Throughout Budapest **TRANSPORT** Kossuth Lajos tér (metro) is a short walk from the Postal Savings Bank; Zugló (train station) is near Szenes House **INFORMATION** Some buildings require a fee to enter (budapestinfo.hu)

You'll find beautiful Art Nouveau buildings all around Europe, but few cities have a collection quite like this. Budapest had an intense – if short-lived – love affair with the movement, and many examples of the style still stand today.

Beginning in Brussels in the 1890s, the Art Nouveau style swept across Europe, pulling numerous cities under its spell (Riga, Prague, Vienna and Glasgow among them). It symbolized a break from more traditional styles, but it also put beauty front and centre – and painters, textile artists, interior designers and architects couldn't get enough.

Hungary's capital was quick to respond to the movement. The city was thriving at the turn of the century: it was part of the wealthy Austro-Hungarian Empire and had grown in size thanks to the union of the areas of Buda and Pest (in 1873). Yet it lacked a distinctive national identity; enter Szecesszió, Hungary's take on Art Nouveau.

The country's architects embraced Szecesszió (which translates to "stepping away") with fervour, but none quite so much as Hungarian architect Ödön Lechner. Nicknamed the Hungarian Gaudí, Lechner designed countless buildings during the movement's golden age, which together gave the Hungarian capital a dazzling new look, and a new identity. These buildings were all in the style of Art Nouveau – with vibrant tiles, curling lines, floral motifs and organic shapes – but Lechner added his own twist, too. Along with more classical elements of the movement, he utilized the rich imagery and colour palette of Hungarian folklore, distinguishing Szecesszió from other countries' Art Nouveau styles.

Some of Lechner's best buildings can be found in the heart of Budapest, but he wasn't the only Hungarian architect with a penchant for the style. Take a walk around the city and you'll pass an array of masterpieces by other Szecesszió-loving architects. With their calligraphic curves, golden embellishments and colourful tiles, these buildings are more than a little spellbinding.

MUST-SEE BUILDINGS

POSTAL SAVINGS BANK
Completed in 1901, this is Lechner's and Szecesszió's most famous building. Its gaudy green-and-gold roof incorporates elements such as bees and snakes, redolent of Hungarian folk art (Hold u 4).

HUNGARIAN GEOLOGICAL INSTITUTE
This 1896 Lechner work features folklore depictions on its tilework and a roof of brilliant blue; the latter represents the Tethys Ocean, which once divided the supercontinent of Pangea (Stefánia út 14).

SZENES HOUSE
A lesser-known Art Nouveau treasure, this apartment block has powder-blue flower embossments and butterfly-shaped balcony guard rails (Thököly út 46-I/9).

MUSEUM OF APPLIED ARTS
This Lechner design has a characteristically elaborate dome-shaped tiled roof (Üllői út 33–37).

REYKJAVÍK • ICELAND

HALLGRÍMSKIRKJA

WHERE Hallgrímstorg 1 **TRANSPORT** Take the bus to Reykjavík Bus Terminal **INFORMATION** Hours vary, check website (hallgrimskirkja.is); fee to climb tower

With a landscape and heritage as epic as Iceland's, why wouldn't you take inspiration from it? Reykjavík's famous church is a human-made homage to Iceland in all its glory.

When it came to designing Iceland's national church, Guðjón Samúelsson, one of the country's most prolific architects, had a clear vision: to showcase what he considered to be Iceland's most iconic features. While the church's shape resembles a giant organ at first glance, the fluted façade also evokes the corrugated basalt rock faces that characterize the island's dramatic scenery, especially the cliffs of talismanic Svartifoss waterfall. The exterior's white granite cast, meanwhile, is suggestive of the churning water and snow that cover much of the land. Then there's the sanctuary, its conical domed shape likened to a typical Viking war helmet, leaning into the country's famous Viking roots. Topping it all off are verses of pastor-poet and national treasure Hallgrímur Pétursson inscribed on the pulpit and font.

A FINE ACHIEVEMENT

The locals have taken a while to fall in love with the church, with many pointing to its "drab" concrete-grey colouration, but there's no argument about this being the city's most interesting building architecturally. At 74 m (243 ft) high, it's also the island's second tallest building (office and retail building Smáratorg Tower in Kópavogur being the first), affording views of the very scenery that inspired its design.

Right The church's distinctive curved spire; its minimalist interior

WHEN TO GO

For a few days in February, the Reykjavík Lights Festival sees bold light installations brighten up the capital's landmarks, including this famous church. Better yet, all events are free to attend; find out more at reykjavik.is.

HEDDAL · NORWAY

HEDDAL STAVE CHURCH

WHERE Heddalsvegen 412 **TRANSPORT** Take a bus from Oslo to Notodden, then a bus to Rygi **INFORMATION** Opening hours vary, check website (heddalstavkirke.no); ticket required

Once upon a time, Norway was home to around 1,000 stave churches – wooden churches supported by pillars, or staves. Of the 28 that remain, this 13th-century beauty is the finest.

From the 11th to 13th centuries, while Europe was using stone to build cathedrals, Norwegians used the natural resources at hand: the forest. Built using the same woodworking skills that the Vikings applied to their longhouses and longboats, these stave churches were wooden monuments to early Norse Christianity, with many preserved and still functioning across Norway today, including Heddal Stave Church – the largest you'll find.

As if plucked straight from a fairytale, Heddal Stave Church rises in steeply gabled waves from surrounding farmland, its intricate, turreted spire soaring 29 m (95 ft) into the sky. Before building commenced around 1200, the wood was cut from the heart of old-growth pine trees and then steeped in resin for 15 or 20 years to make it less susceptible to rot. Construction aside, what makes this place special is the vivid minutiae of the design detail. Likenesses of beasts, probably intended to ward off evil spirits, along with runic inscriptions are carved into the exterior; motifs depicting the bridge between pagan and Christian beliefs, such as those of Sigurd the dragon-slayer, emblazon the furniture inside; and masked faces, believed to be ancestors important to the builders' contemporaries, gaze down from interior column tops. This stave church really is the fairest of them all.

Next page Triple-turreted Heddal Stave Church

AFRICA AND THE MIDDLE EAST

Some of the world's oldest civilizations began in Africa and the Middle East, and the evidence is clear to see. Egypt, for one, is packed with ancient monuments, constructed under the reigns of numerous pharaohs and still standing tall today. Then there's Petra, a sprawling ancient city of colonnaded streets and grand mausoleums, once the capital of the Nabataean Kingdom. But this ancient architecture isn't the region's only story; there are modern landmarks here, too. Marvels like the Zeitz MOCAA and the Mapungubwe Interpretation Centre have put places like South Africa on the map, while super-tall skyscrapers, modern mosques and some of the world's most groundbreaking structures have come to define cities like Dubai and Abu Dhabi. Is this the new home of pioneering architecture? It might well be.

Clockwise from top
The night market at the Jemaa el-Fna; Bab Agnaou, one of the city gates; the elegant Saadian Tombs

34

MARRAKESH · MOROCCO

THE MEDINA OF MARRAKESH

WHERE Central Marrakesh **TRANSPORT** Taxis and local buses run from Marrakech Railway Station or Marrakesh Menara Airport

Few ancient city centres evoke the past as powerfully as this one. Surrounded by hulking walls and packed with bustling markets and elegant mosques, Marrakesh's medina promises heaps of history and plenty of atmosphere.

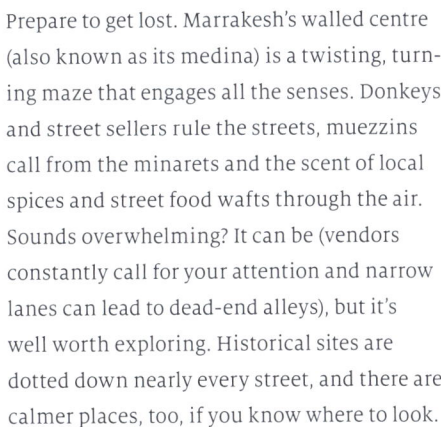

Prepare to get lost. Marrakesh's walled centre (also known as its medina) is a twisting, turning maze that engages all the senses. Donkeys and street sellers rule the streets, muezzins call from the minarets and the scent of local spices and street food wafts through the air. Sounds overwhelming? It can be (vendors constantly call for your attention and narrow lanes can lead to dead-end alleys), but it's well worth exploring. Historical sites are dotted down nearly every street, and there are calmer places, too, if you know where to look.

THOUSAND-YEAR-OLD WALLS

A UNESCO World Heritage Site, this sprawling medina was founded back in 1062 by the Almoravids, an Amazigh Muslim dynasty from the Sahara. They built the city using a local iron-rich clay (pinkish-red in colour) and, most famously, raised the walls that still surround it today. Dating from the 12th century, these hulking walls were originally built as defensive ramparts – Marrakesh has long been an enviable trading centre thanks to its position along trans-Saharan and Mediterranean trade routes, hence the array of souks and the thick walls to protect them. Just like the rest of the medina, they're pinkish-red in colour. Long-standing heritage rules still require new buildings to be built with the same hue.

Once you've passed through one of the city gates, it's time to navigate the medina. Whichever route you take here, you're sure to see something spectacular. It might be the lofty Koutoubia Mosque (you'll spot its minaret from all corners of the medina), the magnificent Saadian Tombs (intricately decorated mausoleums from the 16th century), the bustling souks (trade continues to be the city's mainstay) or the Jemaa el-Fna (which has been the heart of the city for centuries).

AFRICA AND THE MIDDLE EAST   87

Clockwise from top The fortified Aït Benhaddou; the village's red, rammed, earth walls; geometric motifs

35

AÏT BENHADDOU • MOROCCO

KSAR OF AÏT BENHADDOU

WHERE 30 km (19 miles) northwest of Ouarzazate, off road N9
TRANSPORT You'll need to hire a car or take a taxi to reach the village

Perched in the High Atlas foothills like a cluster of children's sandcastles, Aït Benhaddou is Morocco's most iconic *ksar* or *ighrem* (fortified village). Looks familiar? It's had many a starring role on screens both big and small.

Remember Daenerys Targaryen conquering the city of Yunkai in *Game of Thrones*? Or Maximus Decimus Meridius arriving in the town of Zucchabar in *Gladiator*? Both sites were actually Aït Benhaddou. Also appearing in *Lawrence of Arabia*, *The Mummy* and *Kingdom of Heaven*, this historic Moroccan village frequently steals the spotlight on screen.

Tumbling down the red-rock slopes of Morocco's Ounila Valley and perfectly blending with its surroundings, epic Aït Benhaddou looks both ancient and fantastical – of which it's neither. This cinematic village was built along one of the main trans-Saharan trade routes in the 17th century and served as a pit stop for numerous long-distance traders and adventurers, and their camels. By the 20th century, trade had moved on and Aït Benhaddou soon lost its strategic importance; today, it's sparsely inhabited and mainly survives as a tourist attraction (and, of course, film star).

SCENE-BUILDING

The red mass of Aït Benhaddou comprises high defensive walls, kasbahs (castles), houses, a mosque, a public square and a caravanserai (travellers' inn), which fit together like a game of Tetris. It's a striking sight – so neatly stacked and uniformly built – and it's practical, too. Made of rammed earth, clay bricks and wood (materials that are naturally dense in thermal mass), the buildings are set close together for shade, and have small windows to help regulate the temperature, which soars by day and plunges at night. Decoration is minimal, but you'll spot some ornamentation – a crenellated tower here, a geometric motif there.

While these natural materials are pretty and practical, they're not perfect. Weathering is a major issue in Aït Benhaddou, making maintenance a year-round occupation. Luckily, the filmmakers who flock here help out with restoration efforts, too. After all, Aït Benhaddou needs to be ready for that close-up.

PHOTO OPPORTUNITY

For a dramatic view of the entire *ksar*, scattered over its rocky hill, with palm trees or the River Ounila in the foreground, position yourself on the opposite side of the river. In the *ksar* itself, the higher you climb, the better the panoramas.

LIMPOPO · SOUTH AFRICA

MAPUNGUBWE INTERPRETATION CENTRE

WHERE Mapungubwe National Park **TRANSPORT** Taxi from Polokwane International Airport **INFORMATION** Open daily

Taking inspiration from the wild, rocky landscape that surrounds it, Mapungubwe's national park centre is a great example of environmentally conscious modern architecture.

You might not spot it straight away. Blending into the rocks and shrubs of South Africa's Mapungubwe National Park, this understated visitor centre looks more like a collection of rocky hills than an award-winning piece of architecture. But why can't it be both?

Opened in 2009, the Mapungubwe Interpretation Centre serves as a museum and visitor centre for the surrounding UNESCO World Heritage Site, where some of sub-Saharan Africa's most significant Iron Age remains have been found, along with artifacts from the 13th-century Kingdom of Mapungubwe. It was designed by Peter Rich, a celebrated South African architect with a passion for Indigenous culture and history. His economical design called for a cluster of mound-like structures, intended to echo the cairns with which rural Africans mark routes. Inside, timbrel vaulting encloses cavernous exhibition spaces, which are flooded with natural light. Remarkably, everything here was built by hand from local sandstone rocks, using techniques based on ancient local practices: the building's earthen tiles, for example, are unfired and were handmade on site. The construction team also involved unemployed youngsters in the project, teaching them skills they could pass on to their communities. This is a building that's both environmentally and culturally conscious; little wonder, then, that it was awarded World Building of the Year in 2009.

WHEN TO GO
The best time to visit Mapungubwe National Park is during the region's dry season (May to September), when the rains have passed and the temperature isn't too oppressive.

Right Mapungubwe Interpretation Centre, built using local materials

CAPE TOWN • SOUTH AFRICA

ZEITZ MOCAA

WHERE South Arm Rd, Victoria & Alfred Waterfront, Cape Town
TRANSPORT Waterfront Silo is the nearest bus stop
INFORMATION Open 10am–6pm daily; ticket required

Set in Cape Town's semi-regenerated docklands, the austere exterior of Africa's largest contemporary art museum offers few hints of the drama within.

Looming over Cape Town's buzzy Victoria & Alfred Waterfront, this enormous art museum began life as a 1920s-era grain silo, and it still looks like one. From the outside, that is. Inside, it's had a dazzling modern makeover.

Transforming this mammoth industrial building was no small feat. Far from a blank canvas, the warehouse featured a 57-m- (187-ft-) tall tower and a block of 42 massive vertical concrete tubes. It wasn't exactly the ideal space for an art gallery, so Thomas Heatherwick (of acclaimed architectural firm Heatherwick Studio) had to get creative. He carved the gallery's multi-storey atrium (which is fittingly shaped like a grain of corn) out of the concrete tubes, resulting in an intriguing internal landscape of concrete circles, ovals and curves, cleverly lit by daylight. From here, transparent lifts whizz visitors up to the art galleries.

Compared to the atrium, these 100 galleries are more conventional (a network of white cubes in the building's core), but that's the point. With art this good, the architecture takes a back seat. The museum's permanent collection features over 500 objects from Africa and the Diaspora, with work spanning fine art, photography, sculptures and installations. Particular highlights include the collections of two South African artists: Nandipha Mntambo (known for her expressive cowhide sculptures) and Zanele Muholi (famed for their striking black-and-white photography).

Next page The towering Zeitz MOCAA, opened in 2017

AFRICA AND THE MIDDLE EAST

Egypt's iconic three Pyramids of Giza

CAIRO · EGYPT

PYRAMIDS OF GIZA

WHERE Sharia al-Ahram, Giza **TRANSPORT** Taxis or microbuses from Giza metro station can drop you at the main gate **INFORMATION** Open 7am–5pm daily; general entry tickets grant access to the Giza Plateau monuments; there are separate entrance fees for entering the pyramids and certain tombs (egymonuments.gov.eg)

Icons of Egypt, the last remaining wonders of the ancient world and the tallest structures in the world until 1311: the Pyramids of Giza have earned a place on everyone's bucket list.

Few structures capture our collective imagination quite so much as the great Pyramids of Giza. Icons of Egypt, these three stone giants have been plastered on postcards, featured in films and endlessly talked about by archaeologists and historians – even ancient Greek historian Herodotus wrote about them way back in the 5th century BCE (by then they were over 2,000 years old). It's hardly surprising that they've had so much airtime: constructed nearly 5,000 years ago, each pyramid is made up of millions of stones, and rises above the desert plateau. You can't help but ask, how are they so huge? And why were they built in the first place?

Outlandish theories (including ancient aliens) have abounded over the centuries, but the pyramids are generally believed to be burial sites for ancient Egypt's 4th dynasty pharaohs. As for the ins and outs of transporting all those heavy stones, that mystery was largely solved in 2013. Archaeological excavations on Egypt's Red Sea coast unearthed a papyrus logbook, which documented the logistics of transporting huge numbers of limestone blocks by boat from the quarries of ancient Turah to Giza (just outside Cairo). Researchers have also proposed that an ancient tributary of the Nile may have once passed by the site of the pyramids. From the water, the labourers likely moved the blocks along large ramps, using a system of sledges, ropes and levers. Mystery solved? We'll never know for sure.

THE GREAT PYRAMID

The Pyramids of Giza weren't the country's first pyramids (that honour goes to the Step Pyramid of Djoser in nearby Saqqara), but they're easily the most famous. And the most successful. The first was built as a towering tomb for Khufu (second pharaoh of ancient Egypt's 4th dynasty), some time between 2589 and 2566 BCE. When completed, it rose 146.5 m (480.5 ft) tall and its 2.3 million gargantuan stone blocks were clad in blazing

Clockwise from left
The ancient Sphinx; the hulking bricks in Khufu's Great Pyramid; the narrow tunnel to the King's Chamber, in Khufu's pyramid

white Turah limestone. Across the ensuing 46 centuries, that shimmering cladding may have been ransacked and 9 m (30 ft) knocked off its height, but the gobsmacking ambition and architectural legacy of Khufu's Great Pyramid has never been equalled.

AND THEN THERE WERE THREE

Khufu's Great Pyramid wasn't lonely for long. Within a century, the ancient Egyptians had transformed the Giza Plateau into a royal necropolis, home to three grand pyramid complexes for three generations of pharaohs: one for Khufu, one for his son (Khafre) and one for his grandson (Menkaure). And that wasn't all.

Each of the main pyramids is surrounded by cemetery clusters of smaller subsidiary pyramids and mastaba tombs, which belonged to members of the royal family and royal court. Khafre's and Menkaure's pyramids also include funerary temples linked by what would have been monumental causeways. The causeway from Khafre's pyramid trails down to the Sphinx, which most archaeologists believe to have been created during Khafre's reign. Carved out of the bedrock, and towering 20 m (65 ft) tall, this pharaoh-headed lion with outstretched paws is the first example of the kind of gargantuan statuary that Pharaonic Egypt would become famous for. It also had a stylized false beard (a symbol of royalty), but that fell off some centuries ago, along with its nose.

INSIDE THE PYRAMIDS

Nothing quite prepares you for seeing the pyramids in person – they're always bigger than you expect – and venturing inside these ancient tombs is equally thrilling. Steep shafts (claustrophobes, beware) lead deep into the pyramid's granite-block chambers. In the Great Pyramid, the Subterranean Chamber lies 30 m (98 ft) below the plateau's surface, while the red-granite King's Chamber is reached by ascending the 46-m (150-ft)-long corbelled passageway called the Grand Gallery. Of course, there's nothing left inside, bar an empty sarcophagus – tomb raiders plundered the pyramids centuries ago, stealing whatever was inside (ancient artifacts or royal mummies, perhaps). But you're not here to see them anyway. You're here for the last remaining wonder of the ancient world, and what a wonder it is.

📷
PHOTO OPPORTUNITY

The iconic pyramid shot, of all three pyramids lined up together, is taken from the Pyramids Panorama ridge, a 2-km (1-mile) walk south of Menkaure's pyramid.

AFRICA AND THE MIDDLE EAST

Clockwise from top The Great Hypostyle Hall; a statue in the complex; a processional road

LUXOR · EGYPT

KARNAK TEMPLE COMPLEX

WHERE Sharia Corniche Al-Nile, Luxor's east bank **TRANSPORT** Taxis run from central Luxor **INFORMATION** Open 6am–5pm daily; buy tickets at Karnak's entrance

After the Pyramids of Giza, Karnak is arguably Egypt's most important Pharaonic site. This vast religious complex comprises huge holy sanctuaries, towering hypostyle halls and epic statuary – all of which will make you feel very small indeed.

Often called the world's greatest open-air museum, the city of Luxor grew out of the ruins of Thebes. This famed ancient centre became the capital of Egypt during the New Kingdom period (1550–1069 BCE), and for centuries it acted as the country's major political and religious hub. Its venerable past is still clear to see today: Luxor is home to a mind-boggling number of monuments. The highlight, however, has to be Karnak.

Covering over 2 sq km (1 sq mile), this huge religious complex is centred on the grand Temple of Amun, but it also encompasses several separate sanctuaries, temples and a museum, connected by processional roads and framed by soaring pylons (monumental gateways) and colossal statues. The complex was dedicated to the Theban triad of gods – Amun, his consort Mut and their son Khonsu – and for over 1,500 years it stood as the pinnacle of ancient Egypt's artistry. While it was constantly rejigged and redecorated, the grandest building works occurred during the New Kingdom period, as pharaohs of the 18th and 19th dynasties one-upped each other in the form of architectural extravagance.

A STATEMENT OF POWER

The grandest of Karnak's grand monuments, the Temple of Amun was one of the ancient world's most powerful religious hubs (it employed over 80,000 people). Today, this awesome feat of engineering and architecture still stands as one of the greatest sacred buildings ever built – it makes the lofty spired cathedrals of Europe look like humble undertakings in contrast. The site is epic at every turn, but the Great Hypostyle Hall has few rivals when it comes to wow factor. Walk amid this stone forest of gargantuan papyrus columns, all engraved with intricate reliefs, and you'll immediately feel the power of this ancient kingdom. It's indicative of the site as a whole: decorated with the furious artistry that only the pharaohs, wielding such all-encompassing power, could ever achieve.

+ WHILE YOU'RE HERE

A short drive south of Karnak, still on the east bank of the Nile, is Luxor Temple. Like Karnak, this ancient site features a medley of halls, pylons and sanctuaries, which were raised by a roll-call of New Kingdom pharaohs (including Amenhotep III and Ramses II). The city's west bank, meanwhile, is famed for the Valley of the Kings, where some of ancient Egypt's most well-known rulers were buried. Nearby, Hatshepsut Temple (raised by the New Kingdom's female pharaoh, Hatshepsut) is also a must-see.

The Treasury, which famously starred in Indiana Jones and the Last Crusade

WADI MUSA · JORDAN

PETRA

WHERE Tourism St, Lower Wadi Musa **TRANSPORT** Buses run from Amman to Wadi Musa Bus Station or hire a car **INFORMATION** Open Mar–Sep: 6am–6pm daily (Oct–Feb: to 5pm); purchase your entrance ticket in advance (visitpetra.jo)

Carved into the sandstone cliffs of an arid, pink-hued valley, Petra's colossal monuments are some of the world's greatest fusions of nature and architecture. So great, in fact, that this 2,000-year-old rock-hewn city is still standing strong today.

Petra doesn't reveal itself straight away. Before reaching this ancient city, you'll wind through a skinny pink gorge, its weathered walls so high they nearly block out the sky. Known as the Siq, this narrow shaded path makes for an atmospheric entrance to the city, but it seems to go on… forever. With every turn, anticipation builds (everyone is waiting for *that* view) and as you're greeted with more empty rock faces, the 1.2-km- (0.7-mile-) long twisting trail starts to feel more like a maze. But then, finally, there it is: framed by the chunky gorge walls, the iconic Treasury (Al-Khazneh) suddenly appears.

If you didn't know better, you might turn back now. The colonnaded Treasury – actually a mausoleum built for a king – is the most famous image of Petra, but it's not the only monument here. Walk a little further and you'll find yourself in a yawning valley, surrounded by soaring ruins, all whittled out of the rose-tinted cliff faces. There are hundreds (tombs, temples, even an 8,500-seat theatre), and you'll need more than a day to see them all.

DESIGNED FOR THE DESERT

But who built them? Petra was constructed between the 3rd century BCE and the 1st century CE by the ancient Nabataeans. It was the capital of their kingdom and a thriving epicentre of the ancient world's spice and incense trade, due to its location at a key crossroads in the Middle East. Rich from the trade, the Nabataeans crafted vast monuments for their capital (all created using simple chisel and pickaxe tools) and an ingenious water management system (you can see the remnants of this on the walls of the Siq).

The Nabataeans's architecture was inspired by their travels – both the Treasury and the Monastery (Petra's most colossal structure) feature lofty Corinthian columns, but there's also a Roman-style colonnaded street and a Byzantine-era basilica. And that hardly scrapes the surface. Climb to the High Place of Sacrifice for a glimpse into the darker aspects of Nabataean culture or walk around the great Theatre, which hosted musical performances. There's no doubt: this is architecture on an epic scale.

PHOTO OPPORTUNITY

The Sheikh Zayed Grand Mosque is so vast that it can be difficult to photograph as a whole. Head across the road to Wahat Al-Karama Memorial Park to capture the building in its entirety.

Clockwise from top The grand exterior of the mosque; the courtyard's white marble columns; the golden-hued interior

ABU DHABI • UAE

SHEIKH ZAYED GRAND MOSQUE

WHERE Sheikh Zayed bin Rasheed St, Al-Rawdah **TRANSPORT** Make use of the Abu Dhabi free shuttle-bus routes B2, B3, C & E **INFORMATION** Open for non-worshipping visitors 9am–10pm Sat–Thu; 9am–noon & 3–10pm Fri (szgmc.gov.ae)

One of the most opulent examples of modern religious architecture in the world, the Sheikh Zayed Grand Mosque is the UAE's most beautiful building and a reminder of the powerful role that architecture can play in culture.

Architecture in the UAE tends to go big, and Sheikh Zayed Grand Mosque is no different. This is the country's largest mosque (with capacity for over 55,000 worshippers) and one of the largest in the world. It dominates Abu Dhabi Island's eastern edge and is so vast that you'll need to keep stepping back (and back and back) to get a sense of the building's entirety. But it's well worth taking it all in.

Sheikh Zayed Grand Mosque features 96 blinding-white marble domes, 1,096 exterior columns and four lofty minarets – which pierce the sky at 106 m (350 ft) tall. It was built by more than 3,000 workers between 1996 and 2007, using materials from all around the world, including more than 30 types of marble and thousands of semi-precious stones. When it was finally completed, it broke a number of records – here you'll find the world's largest hand-knotted carpet, the largest crystal chandelier and the largest marble mosaic artwork in the world. Walking through its impossibly vast courtyard and its towering halls, you'll feel very small, but it's not all about size here. Beauty also abounds.

The marble courtyard floor is decorated with swirling floral motifs, while the surrounding columns feature an inlaid vine design of semi-precious stones, topped by golden date-palm capitals. Inside, three massive crystal chandeliers (Swarovski crystals, no less), suspended from three domes, mirror the Islamic medallions on the hall's beautiful carpet below. Look a little closer and you'll also spot how the interlocking geometric decoration and marble floral mosaics on the interior walls, plus the Murano glass mosaics on the doors, have been created to illuminate and enhance this mirror-like effect. Islamic architecture is all about symmetry, and it really is beautiful here.

ABU DHABI • UAE

LOUVRE ABU DHABI

WHERE Jacques Chirac St, Saadiyat Island **TRANSPORT** The free city shuttle bus (A1 route) runs to the Louvre; or take a water taxi from Marsa Mina **INFORMATION** Hours vary, check website (louvreabudhabi.ae)

Inspired by tradition yet futuristic in vision, the Louvre Abu Dhabi is a contemporary artistic icon. It's also the Arab world's first universal museum.

Have you ever seen a museum quite like this one? A collaboration between France and the UAE, the Louvre Abu Dhabi hosts a priceless collection of art and artifacts, many loaned from galleries around France (including its namesake, the Louvre). You'll spot figurines from ancient Egypt, Impressionist masterpieces and contemporary installations. But perhaps the most priceless thing here is the building itself.

Designed by Pritzker Prize-winning architect Jean Nouvel, the museum seems to hover above the turquoise Gulf waters, though it's actually supported by four hidden piers. Its medina-like design comprises 55 white cubes, clustered together to form a striking, interconnected city of art. Sounds incredible, right? That's not even the best part. Linking these cubes together is a vast, silvery dome featuring eight interlocking layers of 7,850 star shapes. These stars allow for an ever-changing interplay of light on the cubes beneath, while also simulating the dappling effect of palm tree leaves (used in traditional Gulf buildings to create cooler environments). As a result, the dome both lowers the building's energy use and protects the precious artifacts inside – proof that cutting-edge contemporary architecture can offer more than just wow factor.

PHOTO OPPORTUNITY

It's hard not to find a photogenic spot in this dazzling museum, but for a unique perspective, jump in a kayak. Museum-run tours take to the water around the galleries from Tuesday to Sunday.

Right *The Louvre's striking interior; the vast dome*

DUBAI · UAE

MUSEUM OF THE FUTURE

WHERE Sheikh Zayed Rd **TRANSPORT** Take the metro to Emirates Towers **INFORMATION** Open 9:30am–9pm daily; book tickets in advance (museumofthefuture.ae)

The future is here, and it's magnificent. With its eye-like silhouette and state-of-the-art construction, the Museum of the Future is one of the quirkiest buildings in Dubai.

Perhaps the future isn't all about glassy skyscrapers. Dubai's uber-contemporary Museum of the Future takes the form of a squashed ring doughnut, or a flying saucer crash-landed on top of a grassy mound. It's clad in shimmering stainless steel, and features windows shaped like the words in an Arabic poem, written by Sheikh Mohammed ("We might not live for centuries, but our creativity leaves a legacy long after we're gone"). There's no denying it stands out amid Dubai's forest of super-tall towers, but don't let its lack of height fool you. This is one of the world's most complex structures.

Creating the museum's unique shape – an oval spread across six floors, with a huge off-centre elliptical void in the middle (representing the still-unwritten future) – required the use of 2,400 steel tubes, which criss-cross through the building's frame. This cutting-edge construction took six years, which is pretty long by Dubai standards (a year longer than the towering Burj Khalifa; p108). But it was worth the effort. Opened in 2022, the Museum of the Future has quickly become one of Dubai's top attractions. It's focused on the world as it will be in the year 2071, and many of its exhibits have a space-bound theme, with huge LED and hologram displays exploring topics such as the science of moon colonization and life aboard a space station. The exhibits are great (there's even a hyper-realistic robot), but the building really takes the cake. Walking around its bright-white interior really does feel like stepping into the future.

Next page The torus-shaped Museum of the Future, lit up at night

AFRICA AND THE MIDDLE EAST

The needle-like Burj Khalifa, constructed in just five years

DUBAI · UAE

BURJ KHALIFA

WHERE 1 Sheikh Mohammed bin Rashid Boulevard **TRANSPORT** Burj Khalifa (metro) is the nearest station **INFORMATION** The building is open 24 hours daily; the viewing platform is open 9am–11pm daily (burjkhalifa.ae)

The totemic building of the modern UAE, the Burj Khalifa is an icon of the country's shiny new development. It's also the world's tallest building, dwarfing Dubai's other sky-high structures.

Dubai does not do things by halves. This is the home of the world's biggest shopping mall, largest artificial archipelago and fastest police cars, among dozens of other superlatives. So it's hardly surprising that when Sheikh Mohammed bin Rashid Al Maktoum decided that his emirate needed a symbolic skyscraper, it had to go bigger than any before.

Looming above the city's already sky-high skyline and piercing the clouds at a dizzying 828 m (2,717 ft) tall, the Burj Khalifa is the world's tallest building by a country mile. Standing at its base and gazing upwards – particularly at night when it becomes the world's largest LED screen, lit up with technicolour patterns – is an experience nothing short of epic. Yet the Burj is even more alluring inside. Eleven of its floors are occupied by the ultra-luxe Armani Hotel; At.mosphere, formerly the world's highest restaurant, serves modern French cuisine in the rarefied air of the 122nd floor; and the At the Top viewing platform (still the world's highest observation deck) offers sweeping city-and-desert panoramas from level (deep breath) 148.

With its Tetris-stacked, glass-clad towers and its reaching spire, which at 243 m (797 ft) tall would be a huge skyscraper in its own right, the Burj is a gleaming monument to the progress and ambition of Dubai. Designed by American architect Adrian Smith, it features an anti-glare shield on its glassy exterior (essential in Dubai's desert heat) and irregular staggered tiers to disrupt the effect of strong winds on its upper levels. Despite its futuristic design, though, nature and religious tradition are at the building's heart. Islamic geometric patterns influenced its design, with its towers recalling the spiral minarets of ancient buildings like the Great Mosque of Samarra in Iraq. The Y-shaped floor plan, meanwhile, is inspired by the petals of the Hymenocallis, a flower that blooms in the harsh Arabian Desert – an epithet that could equally be applied to Dubai itself.

ASIA

Line up Asia's most iconic buildings and you'll start to see a pattern. Empires rise – they carve out grand cities and build great structures – and empires fall... and other empires rise in their place. Thankfully, a host of incredible buildings are left behind every time: China's Forbidden City, Cambodia's Angkor Wat, Thailand's Grand Palace, to name a few. But that's not all Asia has to offer. This vast continent is also home to some of the world's most important religious sites. In India, the Golden Temple marks the spiritual centre of Sikhism; in Indonesia, Borobudur rises as the world's largest Buddhist temple; and in Uzbekistan, the Registan stands as one of the most stunning examples of Islamic architecture. And that hardly scratches the surface. Modern masterpieces, symbolizing 20th- and 21st-century boom times, are on the rise here, too.

Right The fluid exterior, which swirls from the ground up

Below Column-free interior

BAKU · AZERBAIJAN

HEYDAR ALIYEV CENTRE

WHERE 1 Heydar Aliyev Ave **TRANSPORT** Nariman Narimanov (subway) is the nearest station; many local buses go directly to the centre **INFORMATION** Open 10am–6pm Tue–Sat (to 5pm Sun); ticket required (heydaraliyevcenter.az)

Rising and falling in seemingly random waves across a park in central Baku, this Zaha Hadid masterpiece envelops a museum, auditorium, library and gallery. The finest of them all? That might just be the soaring, swooping building itself.

Because of its strategic location on the Caspian Sea and its vast oil reserves, the Azerbaijan capital of Baku has long been a desirable city for various empires to rule over, including Soviet Russia. When Baku gained independence from the Soviet Union in 1991, it finally had the chance to take ownership of its image, and its leaders sought to transform it from a post-Soviet city into a modern capital. This started with reinvigorating the skyline; much of the city was dominated by dull high-rises built during Soviet rule. How to start this process of transformation? Call in Zaha Hadid, considered one of the 20th and 21st century's greatest architects.

FUTURE FOCUSED

Hadid was known as the "Queen of Curves" for the way she eschewed conventional building geometry, and she brought her trademark curves to this commission: a cultural centre for art exhibitions, concerts and festivals that would show off Baku's cultural scene. Standing in stark contrast to the rigidity of the city's Soviet-era architecture, the building's white curves twist outlandishly. It's a look that was achieved by using a steel space-frame structure, allowing the shape to take on its undulating contours and remain supported without obviously visible columns. These swirls bring a real flow to the visitor experience inside; you won't come across any sharp corners, so it can be hard to know where one wall ends and another begins. This is a building to journey through, not just a set of rooms to methodically move in and out of.

Since opening in 2012, the Heydar Aliyev Centre has become a visual symbol of the city's transformation, symbolizing progress and modernity. It's influenced many more architectural showpieces in Baku, too, but this is by far the finest. And it might just be Hadid's best work – a pretty big deal for a city that wanted to show the world how forward-thinking it is.

MORE LIKE THIS

Guangzhou Opera House, China
Hadid designed this futuristic performance venue, one of the planet's most iconic opera houses, to look like pebbles being smoothed by the city's Pearl River.

London Aquatics Centre, UK
Nothing curves in quite such a seamless way as water in motion, and Hadid took this idea as inspiration for this state-of-the-art fitness centre, originally built for the city's 2012 Olympic Games.

MAXXI, Italy
The design of this building in Rome – another of Hadid's greatest works – is as radical as the MAXXI institution itself. Set in a futuristic concrete building, it features a gravity-defying overhang and freestanding stairways.

ASIA

WHEN TO GO

Every evening, a brilliant sound-and-light show illuminates the square and its buildings. The show typically starts at 8pm but can run at different times depending on the season, so check with local tour operators ahead of time.

Left *From left to right, Ulugh Beg Madrasa, Tilya Kori Madrasa and Sher-Dor Madrasa*

Below *Tilya Kori's gold mosaic dome*

SAMARKAND · UZBEKISTAN

THE REGISTAN

WHERE Registan St **TRANSPORT** Buses go to Registan ko'chasi on the south side of the square **INFORMATION** There's a fee to enter the square, which gives access to all three madrasas (uzbekistan.travel)

The Registan isn't your average city square. Surrounded by three of the most stunning educational institutions in the Islamic world, it's a living testament to the cultural and intellectual might of Samarkand at its zenith.

With more than 3,000 years of history flowing through its streets, Samarkand is one of the oldest continually inhabited cities in Central Asia. Its location along the Silk Road trading route made it both a crossroads of cultures and a strategic location – it was so important, in fact, that ruler Amir Timur made it the capital of the Timurid Empire in the 14th century.

As well as military achievements, the Timurid Empire was known for its patronage of the arts and sciences, sparking what was known as the Timurid Renaissance. Cities that belonged to the empire, which stretched from Turkey to India, were developed and revamped, but the heaviest investment went into Samarkand – mosques, palaces and gardens were rebuilt to showcase the glory of the empire. Since the Registan, the city's main square, was at the intersection of major trade routes passing through Samarkand, it was the most logical place for the biggest makeover.

A POWERFUL TRIO

To tour the Registan today is to soak up all that the empire stood for: culture, education and beauty. Walk up the steps leading to the square and you'll be confronted by a trio of huge, sturdy madrasas, colleges for studying religion and other subjects. The façades of these structures line three edges of the square, each one tall and intricately decorated.

The oldest madrasa is Ulugh Beg Madrasa, constructed in the early 1400s by astronomer Ulugh Beg. Its huge *pishtaq* (arched gateway) is covered in ornamental tiles, many of which celebrate Ulugh Beg's love of astronomy – look for the depictions of the sky and stars. Mirrored opposite is the 17th-century Sher-Dor Madrasa, featuring a huge portal decorated with two mythical beasts. Completing the trio is Tilya Kori Madrasa. It's the most elaborate of all, home to a shimmering gilded dome outside and bands of Arabic calligraphy, mosaic tiles and a liberal coating of gold leaf inside. The extravagant detail belies its use: it's home to a mosque and student living quarters.

It's easy to lose track of time as you peer closer at the ornate *muqarnas*, decorative niches above the entrances of each building. If you can tear yourself away, don't sleep on the rest of the city – it's a UNESCO World Heritage Site, after all.

Clockwise from left
The High Court of Punjab and Haryana; the Open Hand Monument mounted on a plinth; Palace of the Assembly, with concrete columns

CHANDIGARH · INDIA

CHANDIGARH

WHERE Throughout the city, with the biggest sights in the Capitol Complex
TRANSPORT Take the train from Delhi to Chandigarh Junction Station
INFORMATION Hours vary, check online (chandigarhtourism.gov.in)

Designed from scratch by the forefather of Modernism in architecture, Le Corbusier, the state capital of both Punjab and Haryana has the world's largest collection of Modernist buildings.

"Let this be a new city," stated then President of India, Jawaharlal Nehru, upon laying Chandigarh's foundation stone in 1952, "symbolic of the freedom of India [and] the nation's faith in the future". Seldom have words so astutely summed up such a landmark moment in architecture. Here was India, five years into independence following two centuries of colonial rule, creating an entire city and state capital from scratch – and with the foremost exponent of modern architecture, Le Corbusier, at the helm.

A CITY FOR EVERYBODY

Le Corbusier, along with British husband-and-wife architects Maxwell Fry and Jane Drew, were already prestigious names in Modernist architecture when they were commissioned by the Indian government. Their involvement would turn international eyes on Chandigarh from the off, and, aided by several Indian architects, the city would match the hype.

Le Corbusier designed the city in the image of a human body, symbolizing its function as a place for living, working and caring for oneself. The Capitol Complex, which includes the dramatic concrete sculptural buildings of the Palace of the Assembly, Secretariat and High Court, is the "head" of the city. The main shopping area, Sector 17, is the "heart", which is adjoined by a stretch of green open spaces, the city's "lungs". Then there's the large residential sectors, with neat houses making up the "torso". The roads are the arteries and veins joining it all together.

Chandigarh isn't all function, though – it's playful, too. Take, for example, the city's symbol: the Open Hand Monument, an enormous weathervane shaped as a splayed-open hand. The open hand is a recurring motif in Le Corbusier's work and is representative of peace and unity – something that the first modern city of independent India wholly stands for.

MUST-SEE BUILDINGS

PALACE OF THE ASSEMBLY
Housing legislative chambers, committee rooms and public spaces, this Modernist icon blends Brutalist and Mid-Century styles. The highlight is its arching cement roof *(Capitol Complex, Sector 1).*

TOWER OF SHADOWS
This elaborate arrangement of open concrete blocks was designed to study the sun's movements *(Capitol Complex, Sector 1).*

GOVERNMENT MUSEUM AND ART GALLERY
Made of exposed concrete and brick tile cladding, this cuboidal building holds a collection of art and artifacts *(Sector 10C).*

HIGH COURT OF PUNJAB AND HARYANA
This Brutalist building, made of reinforced concrete, features bold geometric shapes and a vaulted roof *(Capitol Complex, Sector 1).*

Right Resembling a lotus from above

Below The temple, which took a decade to build, and its lawns

NEW DELHI · INDIA

LOTUS TEMPLE

WHERE Lotus Temple Rd, Kalkaji **TRANSPORT** The temple is a short walk from Kalkaji station (metro) **INFORMATION** Open 8:30am–6pm Tue–Sun; free to enter (bahaihouseofworship.in)

One of the most visited religious sites on earth, and the most important place of worship in the Bahá'í faith, the Lotus Temple is a symbol of the peace, purity and resilience of the lotus flower.

There's no flower more sacred than the lotus in Indian tradition. It blooms out of muddy waters, symbolizing purity, while its petals close at night and open at dawn, representing enlightenment and the triumph of light over darkness. It's an interesting shape, too, inspiring architect Fariborz Sahba when he was tasked with designing New Delhi's Bahá'í House of Worship.

More popularly known as the Lotus Temple, this building is made up of 27 huge, curving "petals" of white marble that reach up to the heavens, giving the impression of a flower just about to unfurl. Beyond decoration, the petals actually form the building's structure. The inner nine petals enclose the interior dome, the middle nine provide structural support and the outer nine – which fan out as opposed to curving inwards – act as canopies over the building's nine entrances. The point where the petals meet at the apex of the roof lets natural light stream in, and their tips create a nine-pointed star, a holy symbol for Bahá'í representing perfection and unity. Why always nine, you ask? It's in keeping with the Bahá'í faith's reverence for the number.

Also important to the faith is the validity and acceptance of all religious traditions – it's why you'll hear recitals of passages from the sacred texts of Christianity, Hinduism and Islam here as well as readings from the writings of Bahá'u'lláh, the Iranian mystic who founded the Bahá'í faith in the 19th century. Everyone is truly welcome here: to worship, sit in quiet meditation, wander the leafy grounds or just admire the architecture.

PHOTO OPPORTUNITY

Sunset is a beautiful time to get a shot of the temple. At dusk, stand on the garden pathway that leads to the eastern entrance and capture the setting sun sinking into the crown of the temple, where the marble petals meet.

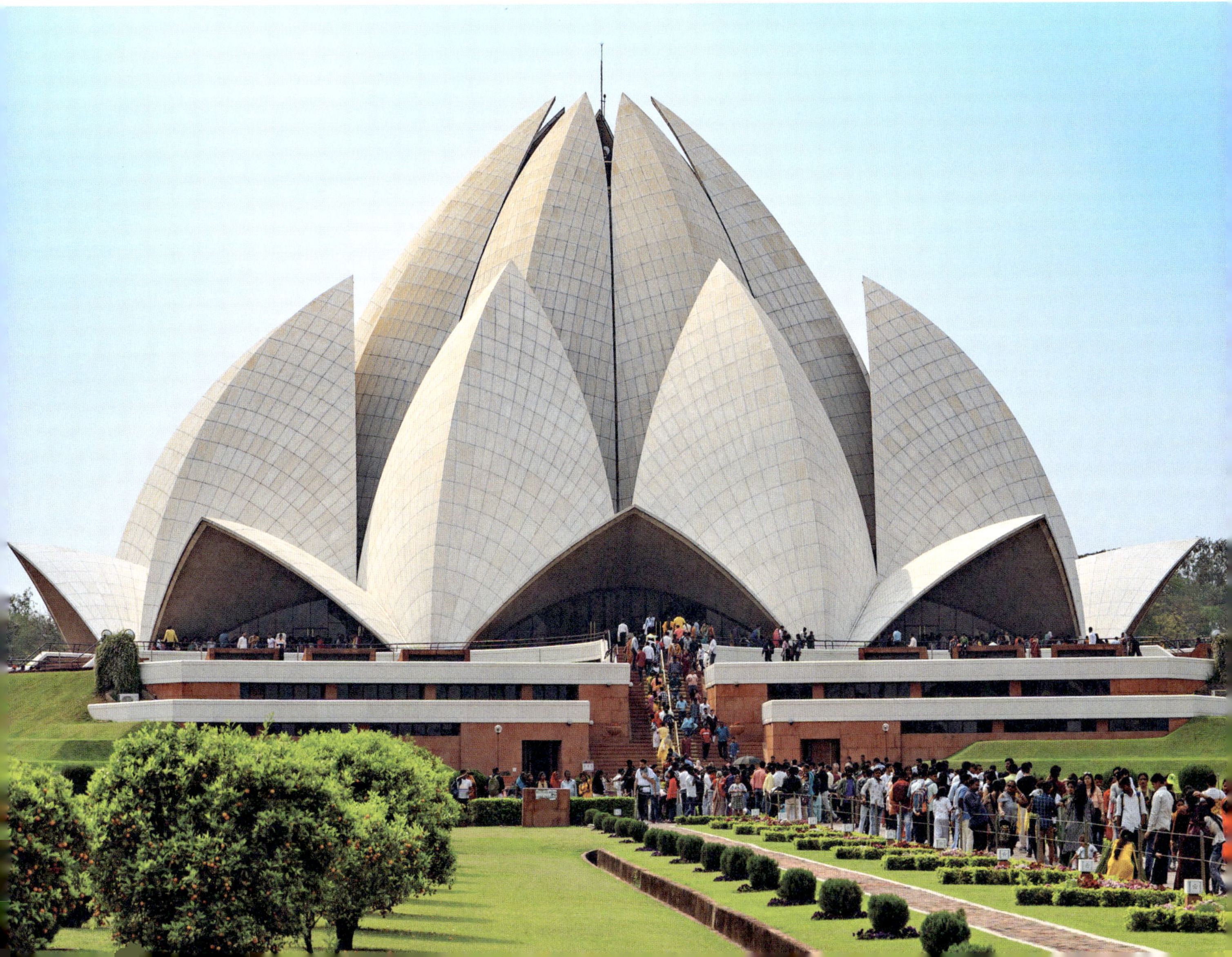

The fort, rising sheer out of a 125-m- (410-ft-) high rock

JODHPUR • INDIA

MEHRANGARH FORT

WHERE Sodagaran Mohalla **TRANSPORT** Trains run to Jodhpur, where autorickshaws take visitors up to the fort (it's also possible to walk) **INFORMATION** Open 9am–5pm daily; ticket required (mehrangarh.org)

The desert forts of Rajasthan evoke a world of powerful emperors, warring kingdoms and camel caravans plodding across ochre sands. Perhaps the most famous is Mehrangarh, a mighty monument of ferrous red sandstone.

Author Rudyard Kipling once described Mehrangarh Fort as being "built by Titans", and it certainly seems possible when you first lay eyes on the forbidding castle, rising sheer out of a 125-m- (410-ft-) high rock. In reality, of course, the fort was built by talented human hands and founded by Jodhpur's founder, Rao Jodha, in 1459. It was added to by later rulers, mostly between the mid-17th and mid-19th centuries, who built palaces, apartments and courtyards within its formidable walls. Because of its strategic position on a huge hill, combined with its towering ramparts and battery of cannons, it stood unconquered for centuries – long enough for the entire city of Jodhpur, now home to 1.6 million people, to grow at its feet.

ALL IN THE DETAIL

Impressive as it may be when looking up at it from Jodhpur, it's actually the little details that make this an outstanding complex. Its forbidding ramparts are in sharp contrast to the flamboyantly decorated palaces within, with their intricate stonework, elegant arches and carved balconies, not to mention the interior rooms inlaid with gold and jewels. The royal apartments form part of a museum today, so take your time admiring these details on a visit. Particular highlights include the 18th-century Phool Mahal, its ceiling decorated with mirrored glass and gold filigree, and the 19th-century Jhanki Mahal, a long gallery with exquisite latticed stone screens. This is a true showcase of what human ambition and artistry can achieve – no Titans required.

WHEN TO GO

Mehrangarh Fort provides a dramatic backdrop to two music festivals each year: the World Sacred Spirit Festival in February *(worldsacredspiritfestival.org)* and the Rajasthan International Folk Festival in October *(jodhpurriff.org)*.

The Taj Mahal, which stands on a 6.5-m- (22-ft-) high platform

AGRA · INDIA

TAJ MAHAL

WHERE Dharmapuri, Forest Colony, Tajganj **TRANSPORT** Taxis or tuk-tuks take visitors to the site, then it's a short walk from the main car park **INFORMATION** Open sunrise to sunset Sat–Thu; ticket required (tajmahal.gov.in)

This could very well be the most famous – and beautiful – building in the world. It's an icon you might think you know, but nothing compares to seeing the details of the Taj Mahal for yourself.

When Mughal emperor Shah Jahan built the Taj Mahal for his beloved late wife, Mumtaz Mahal, he forever raised the bar when it comes to romantic gestures. Completed in 1648, it took over 20,000 labourers and craftspeople 22 years to build this sublime garden-tomb – a symbol of love that beats a bouquet of flowers any day.

A PERFECT DESIGN

When you finally set eyes on this legendary creation, seen so often through paintings, postcards and screens, it doesn't quite look real. This is a building that's so precise and symmetrical, with four minarets framing the tomb on all sides, all of which are beautifully reflected in the long pool below. It gives the impression, from certain angles, that the Taj Mahal is floating in thin air. Get closer and the reality of the building begins to sink in. The pristine white marble is exquisitely decorated, with floral arabesques painted in red and green above ornate screens of latticed stone. Quranic verses are etched into the stone, with text that increases in size as it gets higher, creating the optical illusion of uniform script. The white marble absorbs and transforms in the light, too: rosy pink in the dawn, white and pristine in the noon sun, and ethereal and ghostly in the moon's beams.

The mausoleum is an image so embedded in our popular imagination that it can come as a surprise to learn it's actually the centrepiece of a wider complex that sits within a walled rectangle. West of the mausoleum is a mosque in the red-sandstone Mughal style. On the east side is a *jawab*, which – in keeping with the Taj's commitment to symmetry – is a building that resembles the mosque, though it's purely ornamental, existing only to provide architectural balance. All the buildings are set in manicured gardens, with neat lawns divided into quadrants and lined with pomegranate, cypress and banyan trees.

Above left *The reflecting pool*

Above right *Marble, which came from Makrana in Rajasthan*

AN INSIDE LOOK

These other buildings don't, however, detract from the white-marble mausoleum, the undisputed highlight of the complex. You'll likely be delighted, as many first-time visitors are, to find that you can step inside the Taj itself (you'll just need to buy a second ticket alongside the ticket for the outer complex). And the interior is just as spectacular as the exterior, decorated as it is with precious stones, calligraphic panels and intricate filigree screens. Once inside, it's hard not to be moved by the sight of Mumtaz Mahal's tomb sitting alongside that of Shah Jahan himself (the Mughal emperor outlived his wife – who died at the age of 38 while giving birth to their 14th child – by 27 years). Their tombs are simple and unadorned, in poignant contrast to the ornately latticed stone and geometric carvings of the temple's marble walls and arches.

AN ENDURING LEGEND

Beauty on this scale feels almost mythical, so it's no surprise that a rich body of legends and folk tales have sprung up around the monument. The most persistent is that Shah Jahan had planned to build a negative mirror image of the building – a Black Taj mausoleum – in dark marble on the opposite bank of the Yamuna River, but he

was overthrown by his son Aurangzeb before he could realize his plans. Other legends claim that the Taj Mahal was actually originally a Hindu temple, and that hundreds of architects and stonemasons were killed by Shah Jahan during the creation of the building when they fell short of his standards in his relentless pursuit of perfection.

While no evidence for any of these stories exists, they certainly show the potent sway that the Taj Mahal holds over our imaginations. But, really, this masterful piece of architecture has no need for such flights of fancy – this place is the stuff of legend in its own right.

PHOTO OPPORTUNITY

Hoping to get a picture of the building with hardly a tourist in sight? Capture the view from Mehtab Bagh, a public garden across the Yamuna River from the Taj. It's open from sunrise to sunset, so you can get those gorgeous golden-hour shots.

Above left One of the ornamental minarets

Above right The marble tombs inside the Taj

Clockwise from top
The intricate Kandariya Mahadev Temple; hundreds of carved figures; details on Lakshmana Temple

51

CHHATARPUR · INDIA

KHAJURAHO

WHERE Chhatarpur district **TRANSPORT** Khajuraho has a railway station, bus terminal and small airport **INFORMATION** Open sunrise to sunset daily, though specific temple opening hours may vary; ticket required (mptourism.com)

What makes this temple complex stand out in a country that's home to so many? Its unexpected, imaginative and often gravity-defying sculptures, some of the most intricate and erotically charged in South Asia.

Was it a how-to guide inspired by the Kama Sutra? A representation of Shiva and Parvati's wedding celebrations? Entertainment for the gods? Or a complex for a religious group that regarded sex as a form of worship? There are various theories for why the ancient temples of Khajuraho are covered with depictions of amorous individuals, couples, trios and groups in a dazzling array of positions, poses and combinations. The lack of a definitive answer only adds to the seduction of this site.

What we know for certain is that the temples (for the Hindu and Jain faiths) were built by the influential Chandela dynasty between the 10th and 11th centuries. They were later abandoned and swallowed up by the jungle, which helped to protect them from treasure hunters and iconoclasts, before being excavated from the 19th century. Divided into three main groups, the 25 temples that remain today are the pinnacle of North Indian temple architecture, and none more so than the towering Kandariya Mahadev. It was designed to resemble the sacred Mount Kailash, its main spire surrounded by smaller ones to create the impression of a mountain range. The harmonious composition aside, it is, of course, the decorations that stun the most: more than 800 sculptures depicting gods, warriors, animals and those lustful beings.

INTRICATE FIGURES

The scenes leave little to the imagination, but the intention wasn't for jaws to drop – the sculptures are a display of the artistry that flowered under Chandela rule. At the Lakshmana Temple, figures dance with castanets; at Vishwanath Temple, a celestial nymph plays the flute; and at the Jain Parsvanatha Temple, nymphs apply kohl around their eyes. Visit at sunrise or sunset to really appreciate the detail, when the honey-coloured stone is bathed in a soft light that brings the entangled limbs and ecstatic expressions of the figures to life. They might spark some inspiration.

The Golden Temple, floating in Amritsar Sarovar

AMRITSAR · INDIA

GOLDEN TEMPLE OF AMRITSAR

WHERE Atta Mandi, Katra Ahluwalia **TRANSPORT** Trains run to Amritsar, where taxis to the temple are readily available **INFORMATION** 24 hours daily; free to enter (goldentempleamritsar.org)

The spiritual centre of the Sikh religion, the Golden Temple is one of the holiest places in India, visited by thousands of pilgrims daily. No matter your faith, the sight of the temple shimmering in its reflecting pool is incredible.

As the name indicates, the Golden Temple of Amritsar is pretty lavish: 750 kg (1,650 lb) of gold cover its four squat walls and the domes that crown its roof. But this isn't just a beautiful building – it's also the most important site in Sikhism.

A SPACE FOR ALL

In keeping with Sikhism's tolerant ethos, the temple is open to people of all faiths and backgrounds. Visitors do need to respect certain rituals when here, though, which include removing shoes, washing their feet and covering their heads before entering.

Visits begin with a walk along a 60-m- (197-ft-) long causeway, said to represent the journey of the soul from the mundane to the sacred. And nothing is more sacred than what lies within the temple: the Guru Granth Sahib, Sikhism's holy book, which is displayed under an ornate, jewelled canopy in the main hall. As part of a daily ritual, the book is carried out of the temple at daybreak, when the head priest opens it to read the message for the day. The temple then echoes with the music of ragis, musicians who sing verses from the book, until late at night.

It's a beautiful soundtrack to a temple tour, which starts as soon as you reach the main dome, covered in 100 kg (220 lb) of gold and shaped like an inverted lotus. The interior is just as dazzling, its marble walls decorated with *pietra dura*: semi-precious and precious stone inlays.

Sikhism's warrior tradition is on display here, too, with guards clutching fierce-looking spears. But they're a friendly bunch, often sharing a laugh and a joke with visitors as they pose for photos. It sums up what this temple is all about: bringing joy to all who visit. In fact, like all Sikh gurdwaras, a giant *langar* (dining hall) – the biggest community kitchen in the world – offers free vegetarian food to everyone. This is a golden temple through and through.

Clockwise from left One of 14 gopurams; stucco carving of Shiva; Aayiram Kaal Mandapam

53

MADURAI · INDIA

MEENAKSHI TEMPLE

WHERE Chitrai St **TRANSPORT** Take a local bus or taxi to the streets outside the temple walls **INFORMATION** Open 5am–12:30pm & 4–10pm daily; the main shrines can only be entered by Hindus (meenakshiammantemple.com)

Sprouting from the streets of Madurai, the lofty *gopurams* of Meenakshi Temple – itself a profusion of jasmine garlands, candle-lit halls and barefoot pilgrims – guard one of India's largest Hindu shrines.

Every day, 15,000 devotees make the pilgrimage to Meenakshi Temple, one of the largest Hindu temples in Tamil Nadu. It's also one of the few dedicated to a female deity: the fish-eyed goddess Meenakshi, an incarnation of Hindu goddess Parvati, whose shrine lies at the centre of the complex alongside her consort Sundareśvarar, an incarnation of senior Hindu deity Shiva.

There's evidence a temple stood here in the 6th century CE, but most of what's seen today was added much later during the 17th-century Nayak dynasty, whose religious devotion was backed by piles of cash. The result of all that devotion and money is a showcase of ancient Indian artistry.

DAZZLING PYRAMIDS

Visitors see the towers looming over central Madurai long before they get to the temple entrance. Guarding the main gates are 14 pyramid-like *gopurams*, the tallest of which rises over 52 m (170 ft), their summits the realm of sharp-eyed kites and vultures. Each one is smothered in brightly painted stucco deities, demons and other mythological figures; there are great sinewy serpents, multi-armed dancing gods, deities riding holy bulls, and legendary birds and beasts soaring high above the city.

Inside the temple, there's nothing quite so spectacular, but the Aayiram Kaal Mandapam is worth lingering over. Dubbed the "hall of a thousand pillars", it actually contains 985 pillars, all of which are intricately carved with sculptures of deities and mythical creatures from the Hindu epics. Some pillars even produce clear musical notes when tapped, 500 years after their creation – you'll see plenty of locals trying this, so have a go yourself.

Despite its architectural wonders, this temple isn't a tourist attraction. This is a living, sacred site where the faithful come to pray, so retain a respectful silence when you come across a ceremony.

PHOTO OPPORTUNITY

Photography is forbidden inside the main sanctums, but for a small fee you're able to shoot in most outer areas. Focus on the detail of the *gopurams*: stucco figures depict animals and deities, including a carving of Hindu god Shiva with his 18 hands.

ASIA

TIANJIN · CHINA

TIANJIN BINHAI LIBRARY

WHERE 347 Xusheng Lu, Binhai New Area
TRANSPORT Shimin Guangchang is the nearest station (metro) **INFORMATION** Open 9:30am–8pm daily

This library is more than just an architectural statement – it's a monument to the value placed on knowledge in Chinese culture.

Is this the world's coolest library? It could very well be. Splashed across the social feeds of everyone who walks through its doors, the Tianjin Binhai Library feels less like a civic library and more like something dreamed up by aliens from a distant planet. It was actually conceived by Dutch architecture firm MVRDV along with the Tianjin Urban Planning and Design Institute, and opened in 2017.

AN INGENIOUS DESIGN

The star of this building is the interior, where a huge atrium rises with rippling floor-to-ceiling shelves, each stacked with books to create the illusion of infinity. At the centre floats a spherical orb that has earned the building its nickname, Muzhiguang, or the "Eye of Wisdom". In fact, the building is designed to look like a giant eyeball from the outside, with an oval shape punched through the exterior that looks through to the iris-like spherical orb.

Your own eyes may well deceive you here. While the shelves look endless, many are filled with printed panels rather than real volumes, placed far beyond reach to preserve the illusion. Within the spherical orb is an auditorium with seating for 100 people, too. Wander the terraces, pose against the endless curves and stand beneath the "Eye of Wisdom" to soak in the scale of it all; then, maybe, choose a book to read.

PHOTO OPPORTUNITY
To capture the building's resemblance to an eye, visit at night when the interior is illuminated and stand at a distance outside. Look through the oval shape punched through the exterior to see the central orb glowing from afar.

Right The library's exterior; shelves radiating out from the orb

SHANGHAI · CHINA

SHANGHAI TOWER

WHERE 501 Yincheng Rd, Lujiazui, Pudong **TRANSPORT** Lujiazui (metro) is the nearest station **INFORMATION** Open 8:30am–10pm (last entry: 9:30pm); ticket required

A shiny tube of glass and steel twisting above the clouds, China's tallest building was built to be a showstopper – and it certainly delivers on that.

Shanghai's ultramodern Pudong district was already skyscraper-heavy when San Francisco-based architecture firm Gensler was tasked with creating something extra special. The goal? A building to top all the rest and establish China as a global superpower.

It's safe to say it made a statement when it opened in 2015. The world's third tallest building at a mind-bending 632 m (2,073 ft), Shanghai Tower is mighty in size. But it's also mighty when it comes to sustainability. Gensler's innovative design called for nine cylindrical sections wrapped in two layers of glass, a "double-skin façade" that helps to reduce energy consumption. Uniquely, the tower twists as it rises, a feature that reduces wind shear by almost 25 per cent (and also looks very cool, like a dragon's tail curving into the sky). Its "green" elements set a new standard, using rainwater, wastewater, wind turbines and insulating glass.

A NEED FOR SPEED

Facts and figures aside, this building is simply a thrill to visit. After exploring the exhibition hall on floor B1, step into the world's fastest elevators, travelling at a speed of 20.5 m (67 ft) per second to reach the 118th-floor observation deck – it takes a total of 55 seconds. From here, at a gut-wrenching 546 m (1,791 ft) high, the whole of Shanghai is laid out before you, the ships on the Huangpu River tiny blips on a blue ribbon below. A building that tops the rest, you say? Goal achieved.

Next page The Shanghai Tower on the far left, home to 127 floors

ASIA

56
BADALING/MUTIANYU • CHINA

GREAT WALL OF CHINA

WHERE Well-preserved sections are located in China's Yanqing and Huairou districts **TRANSPORT** Trains and tourist buses run from Beijing **INFORMATION** Typically open 7am–6pm; tickets required, buy on-site or in advance (en.mutianyugreatwall.com)

From the misty hills of Liaoning, near the Korean border, to the sunburned deserts of Gansu in the west, the Great Wall of China sprawls across this country's vast and varied landscapes, and more than lives up to its name.

Clockwise from left Crenellations on the wall; a signal tower; the wall winding through the mountains

An emblem of China and source of national pride, the Great Wall is one of the most impressive works of humankind. It snakes across the hills and plains of this epic country like a sleeping dragon, measuring a staggering 21,196 km (13,171 miles) and crossing 15 provinces and 23 degrees of longitude. It's so immense that when the sun sets at the eastern end of the wall, it takes another two hours until it sets over the western end.

RAISING THE WALL
Despite common misconceptions, the Great Wall was never a single, neat line. Instead, it was a vast system of fortifications built and patched together over centuries. There are parallel ramparts from different eras, branching spurs, lonely signal towers and countless watchtowers and forts once garrisoned by thousands of soldiers. Combined, it traced the uneasy border between the settled Chinese world and the roving horse-mounted tribes from the grasslands to the north.

China's first emperor, Qin Shi Huang, created the first truly "great" wall by unifying existing regional ramparts in the 3rd century BCE. Successive dynasties added to, abandoned or shifted the line, depending on the pressure from the north. Wherever possible, the route was bent to exploit steep ridges, cliffs and rivers, incorporating the landscape into its defence. It was the Ming dynasty, reeling from Mongol incursions in the 14th century, that undertook the grandest wall-building programme of all. Over 6,000 km (3,700 miles) of battlements, bastions and beacon towers were laid out in brick and stone and bound together with mortar mixed with sticky rice.

Militarily redundant since the Qing took power in the 17th century, the Great Wall has since been at the mercy of decay. Yet many of the sturdy Ming sections stand strong today and have become the defining images of the wall. Head to Badaling and Mutianyu (near Beijing) to prowl these iconic defences and look out to the lonely mountains beyond.

PHOTO OPPORTUNITY

For classic shots of the Ming dynasty Great Wall snaking through rugged mountains, but without the tourist crowds, head to any of the watchtowers at Jinshanling, about 125 km (78 miles) northeast of Beijing.

The near 900 buildings of the palace complex

BEIJING · CHINA

THE FORBIDDEN CITY

WHERE 4 Jingshan Front St, Dongcheng **TRANSPORT** The nearest metro stations are Tiananmen Xi and Tiananmen Dong **INFORMATION** Open Apr–Oct: 8:30am–5pm Tue–Sun (Nov–Mar: to 4:30pm); buy tickets online in advance (intl.dpm.org.cn)

Nestled in the heart of Beijing, this gigantic walled palace was once ruled by lofty emperors and was very much off-limits to the public. Today, its historic halls, temples, gardens and courtyards are visited by an average of 15 million people a year.

You can't visit Beijing without visiting the Forbidden City. The capital's most famous monument, this historic site is the world's largest still-standing royal palace. It's also considered the most valuable real estate in the world.

Operating between 1420 and 1912, the Forbidden City was the stage on which China's emperors ruled – 24 of them called the complex home. The palace was built in the very heart of Beijing and enclosed by 3.5 km (2 miles) of walls, which in turn were once surrounded by the walls of the Imperial City and finally Beijing's mighty outer walls. Like Russian nesting dolls, these compass-perfect, symmetrical layers followed ancient feng shui and Confucian principles, placing the emperor at the symbolic centre of the universe, and shaping Beijing into a living expression of imperial power and cosmic order. For almost five centuries, the complex was off-limits, hidden from the public and only accessible to royals, their families and legions of servants and concubines. But today, it's open for all.

INSIDE AN ICON

The Forbidden City is so large that even walking around its vast complex hardly gives a sense of its otherworldly scale. So, picture this: some 900 red-walled buildings, topped with sloping, yellow-tiled roofs; inside, close to 10,000 rooms. As you'd expect, it took a vast workforce (hundreds of thousands of labourers and artisans) to complete the site, and enormous trees were even floated in along rivers from distant jungles to be used as columns for the halls. But the work didn't stop there. Restoration and repair has been perpetual: the entire complex was periodically inundated by fire, and many halls are Qing-era rebuilds (17th and 18th centuries). Even today, fresh lacquer shines and newly restored parts of the palace open to visitors every few years.

To enter the complex, you'll pass through the hulking Meridian Gate, its central arch

Clockwise from left
Colourful arches; the moat surrounding the complex; a mythological creature atop a roof in the city

previously reserved for the emperor. Once inside, you'll see the Golden Water River, crossed by five marble bridges that channel visitors across the vast space towards the Gate of Supreme Harmony. Beyond lies an even larger courtyard; here, thousands of officials, soldiers and attendants once gathered for grand ceremonies. All of them would face north towards the Forbidden City's most spectacular building, the Hall of Supreme Harmony. Raised on a three-tiered white-marble terrace shaped like the Chinese character for "king", it housed the Dragon Throne. From here, the emperor presided as his subjects kowtowed, touching their foreheads to the ground nine times in reverence.

Yet for all the Forbidden City's tremendous scale, it's the small details that are particularly revealing. Look up at the sweeping roof ridges and spot rows of tiny ceramic guardians leading the imperial dragon. Most buildings have nine, but the Hall of Supreme Harmony alone breaks the rule with ten – an exclusive mark of its status. The glazed tiles on the roofs are yellow, a colour reserved for the emperor, while the wooden halls are built without nails, instead using joints that allowed them to flex during earthquakes.

THE EMPEROR'S WORLD

North of the central halls lies a denser world of courtyards and private apartments. This was where the emperors lived, and where the business of ruling China mingled with the rhythms of family life. The spaces are (slightly) more human in scale, but no less beautiful: lacquer gleams under deep eaves, and shadowed colonnades give way to sudden pockets of light. At the far end lies the Imperial Garden, a shady square of pavilions, rockeries and ancient cypresses as knotted as calligraphy. After walking through seemingly endless courtyards and halls, it's the ideal place to rest, as the emperors before you once did.

PHOTO OPPORTUNITY

For the ultimate photo of the Forbidden City, you don't even need to enter the complex. Instead, go to Jingshan Park and climb up to Wanchun Pavilion. From there, you can capture the entire complex.

WHEN TO GO

Avoid visiting during Chinese New Year or the first week of October (National Day holidays), when domestic crowds can be overwhelming. Weekdays in spring or autumn are far calmer and more pleasant for exploring the vast site.

SEOUL · SOUTH KOREA

GYEONGBOKGUNG PALACE

WHERE 161 Sajik-ro, Jongno District **TRANSPORT** It's a short walk from Gwanghwamun metro **INFORMATION** Hours vary, check website (royal.khs.go.kr); last admission one hour before closing; tickets can be bought on-site

Meet Seoul's stunning survivor. This stately palace complex was raised by the first of Korea's foremost royal dynasty, revived by the last and ravaged by war and invasion. Now it's undergoing one of the world's biggest restoration projects.

Right Gwanghwamun Gate, the entrance to the palace

Below The feng shui-inspired layout

The roots of one-time royal residence Gyeongbokgung Palace trace back to the roots of Seoul itself. The city became capital of what is now Korea in 1394 under King Taejo of the Joseon dynasty. The palace was then raised in 1395 and given a name meaning "a new dynasty shall prosper", and for the most part it was accurate – the Joseon dynasty ruled for the next 500 years. The history of Gyeongbokgung itself is rockier. The palace was destroyed during the Japanese invasion of 1592 and remained a ruin until 1867, when it was restored. It then faced large-scale destruction during the Japanese colonial period, when many of its buildings were torn down. A massive restoration project began in the 1990s, which is ongoing, but visitors can still walk around this historic royal residence.

It's a calming place to wander, largely thanks to the feng shui principles the site's layout follows, with multiple buildings neatly arranged within a large walled courtyard. Its design, meanwhile, is a coalescence of Chinese and Korean influences – marks of the Ming dynasty can be seen in the gracefully upturned roofs, while Korean character is on display on the roofs' undersides: *dancheong* paintwork features symbols to ward off evil spirits. The palace retains many original features, too, like the Gyeonghoeru Pavilion and its surrounding ornamental lake, which date to the 1400s. The highlight is easily Geunjeongjeon Hall. This 1395-era hall hosts a dazzling red, blue and green recessed ceiling centred on two dragons (representing kings, fighting for a jewelled ball). Beneath sits the throne upon which seven Joseon monarchs were crowned. It's a mighty room, fit for a mighty dynasty.

WHEN TO GO

The Royal Culture Festivals in May and October are the best times to learn about and enjoy Seoul's palaces, with a varied programme of events.

MORE LIKE THIS

Deoksugung Palace, South Korea
One of Seoul's quintet of Joseon palaces, this synthesis of Korean and Western Neo-Classical styles was first used as a royal palace in 1592.

Changgyeonggung Palace, South Korea
This vast Seoul palace complex and erstwhile royal residence dates to the 15th century; it benefitted from a renovation in the 17th century.

Hwaseong Fortress, South Korea
Just outside Seoul, the town of Suwon is wrapped by the stunning, UNESCO-listed Hwaseong Fortress. The building was completed in 1796.

The Golden Pavilion, a glimmering legacy of medieval Japan

KYOTO · JAPAN

TEMPLES OF KYOTO

WHERE Throughout Kyoto **TRANSPORT** Trains go to Kyoto Station from many parts of Japan, including Osaka

The imperial capital for more than a thousand years, Kyoto has over a thousand temples to show for it – the finest in Japan, for that matter. A tour of as many of them as possible, then, is a must.

Japan has no shortage of historic temples, but if pressed to choose where the very best (and most important) lie, it'd be in the ancient capital of Kyoto. In 794, Kyoto (then Heian-kyō) became Japan's imperial capital, kick-starting a building boom that would result in an eventual 1,600 temples. Today, these famous monuments are preserved in and around a lively modern city, and all showcase centuries of artistic brilliance and traditional design, from the monumental grandeur of early Buddhist halls to the quiet restraint of Zen spaces. They're all a little different, but there are some key defining features: curving roofs, elegant pagodas and the use of natural textures.

BUDDHIST BEGINNINGS

Given how many temples Kyoto is home to, you'll stumble across one at nearly every corner. But if you want to see the best on your visit to the city, spend some time properly getting to know a select few. One of the most important lies mere minutes away from Kyoto's Modernist train station: the UNESCO-listed To-ji. It's the history of this temple that impresses the most; built in 796, it's one of the oldest in the city, and it's where Kyoto's religious foundations were laid.

Echoes of bygone rituals seem to linger in the Buddhist temple's hallowed halls, which you can explore on a self-guided tour. The two-storey Kondo (main hall) is the highlight, its present structure dating from 1603 (though it was rebuilt in 1644). It's considered a masterpiece; at 57 m (187 ft), the five-storey pagoda is the tallest wooden pagoda in Japan and has become a symbol of Kyoto.

SPACE TO CONTEMPLATE

To-ji paved the way for the building of many other elegant Buddhist temples, including more restrained Zen Buddhist temples. As the name implies, Zen temples favour simplicity and contemplation, and they were built to transport worshippers from the earthly

world to that of the Buddha. Northeast of To-ji lies one of the finest of such temples, Ginkaku-ji, nicknamed the Silver Pavilion. Originally built in the 15th century as a retirement villa for shogun Yoshimasa, it blends residential and religious elements, using white plaster, aged timber and shingled roofing to evoke *wabi-sabi*, the beauty of imperfection. Its garden of neatly raked sand mounds and mossy groves transforms the grounds into living art – some regard it as an unequalled masterpiece of garden design. It'd be easy to spend hours contemplating in these grounds – exactly the intention behind Zen Buddhist temples.

DESIGNED TO IMPRESS

As you explore Kyoto further, you'll come across temples that are just as subdued as Ginkaku-ji, as well as plenty that were clearly built to impress. None feel quite as showy as Kinkaku-ji, more famously known as the Golden Pavilion. A glimmering legacy of medieval Japan, it was built as a retirement villa for Yoshimitsu, the third Ashikaga shogun, who directed that the finished complex become a temple after his death.

The approach to the temple is along a tree-shaded path, which emerges into a bright garden facing the fabled pavilion. An exact replica of the original, which was destroyed by arson in 1950, the three-storey structure gives the temple its famous nickname – it's covered in gold leaf, its silhouette reflecting in the pond in front. While you can't go inside the temple, you can explore its grounds at leisure – the garden is especially beautiful, with Mount Kinugasa serving as a backdrop.

SACRED SPACES

Stunning as the temples you'll come across are, remember they're all active religious sites, so it pays to be respectful and mindful of how you're behaving when visiting. The golden rules? Don't get in the way of people practising their religion, remove your shoes when entering sacred buildings and keep an eye out for signs saying not to take photos (you might be too distracted by the beauty of the temple to get your phone out, anyway).

Given that Kyoto is home to 1,600 temples, it's worth adopting a Zen mindset here and accepting that you simply can't see all of them in one visit. Instead, embark on a guided tour (you'll find plenty around the city) or spend each day you're here exploring a different part of the city. Who knows what storied temple you'll stumble across?

WHEN TO GO

Visit in October to catch Jidai Matsuri (Festival of the Ages), one of Kyoto's most spectacular festivals. It celebrates the city's heritage with a parade, temple ceremonies and pageantry.

Clockwise from right
The gorgeous hilltop Kiyomizu-dera Temple; borrowed scenery at Tenryu-ji; Ginkaku-ji, also called the Silver Pavilion, though it was never covered in silver foil

MUST-SEE TEMPLES

TO-JI
Kyoto's oldest temple, with its iconic five-storey pagoda, was once a major centre for Shingon Buddhism *(1 Kujocho, Minami)*.

KIYOMIZU-DERA
The wooden veranda of this temple is perched high up on a hillside, from which you'll get sweeping views of Kyoto *(1–294 Kiyomizu, Higashiyama)*.

CHION-IN
The head temple of the Jōdo (Pure Land) sect is home to the towering Sanmon Gate, which rises up to 24 m (79 ft) – the largest of its kind in Japan *(400 Rinkacho, Higashiyama)*.

GINKAKU-JI
Built as a retirement villa for shogun Yoshimasa, the so-called Silver Pavilion later became a Zen temple *(2 Ginkakujicho, Sakyo)*.

TENRYU-JI
Founded by the first Ashikaga shogun, Takauji, in 1339 in memory of Emperor Go-Daigo, this temple is known for its serene gardens and vast pond *(68 Susukinobaba-cho, Saga-Tenryuji)*.

ASIA

The main donjon of Himeji Castle standing proud above the city

HIMEJI · JAPAN

HIMEJI CASTLE

WHERE 68 Honmachi **TRANSPORT** Himeji is the nearest station, then it's a 15–20 minute walk or a quick bus ride **INFORMATION** Open 9am–5pm daily (to 6pm May–Aug); ticket required (himejicastle.jp)

The most spectacular of Japan's 12 still-intact, feudal-era castles, Himeji soars like a heron, its white plaster silhouette said to resemble a bird taking flight. But it's not just easy on the eye; such beauty conceals brilliant military engineering.

Constructed in 1609, Himeji Castle symbolized Japan's new unity under Tokugawa Ieyasu, the first shogun of a long-lasting peace after centuries of civil war. Luck has been on its side ever since; it's still remarkably intact, having somehow survived fires, natural disasters and wars.

WITHSTANDING ATTACK

Though it never saw major battles, the ingeniousness of its defences is woven seamlessly into its architecture. Approaching the keep entails a disorienting, spiralling ascent through narrow gates and high-walled courtyards, leaving attackers at the mercy of hundreds of arrow and gun slits. If they got as far as the keep, their first obstacle would've been the fan-shaped walls, designed to be hard to climb. Then there are the concealed *ishiotoshi* (stone-drop windows), which allowed defenders to drop rocks, boiling oil and water on the heads of invaders. If attackers managed to get through all that to the main donjon, the 45-m- (148-ft-) tall white castle keep, they'd be none the wiser to secret rooms from which defending soldiers could burst forth. From the outside, it appears to have five floors, but inside you discover six: another deliberate trick to confuse attackers.

All that being said, the castle is not a typical feudal fortress. Its 83 buildings and elegant grounds are tranquil spaces to explore, and the interior remains largely unadorned, mostly housing exhibits relating to castle life. The castle highlight? The uppermost chamber, where panoramas over Himeji await.

WHEN TO GO

Visit in early April to catch around 1,000 cherry trees in full bloom across the castle grounds. A little later, in mid-May, the three-day Himeji Castle Festival features historical re-enactments and a costumed procession.

Right The unusually shaped building, with its geometric design

Below The light-filled interior, key to Kahn's design

DHAKA · BANGLADESH

NATIONAL ASSEMBLY BUILDING

WHERE Dhaka 1207 **TRANSPORT** Book a private taxi or take a bus from anywhere in Dhaka **INFORMATION** Open 11am–4pm Sun–Thu; admission is by guided tour only, apply in advance (parliament.gov.bd)

Built to house Bangladesh's parliament, Dhaka's bold National Assembly Building has become something far greater – a Modernist icon that embodies the nation itself.

No building better embodies the history of Bangladesh than the National Assembly Building. Like Bangladeshi history itself, though, its story is complicated. When it was commissioned in 1962, Bangladesh was still part of Pakistan. The ruling military government felt that the rising Bengali independence movement would be placated by making Dhaka the country's second capital and by building this grand civic monument. It didn't work. When the building was finished in 1982, Bangladesh had been an independent country for 10 years, and the building instead came to represent a new nation.

A THOUGHTFUL DESIGN

Designed in signature style by celebrated American architect Louis Kahn, this building is a hulking Modernist monolith. From the outside, the bare, unclad walls reveal their reinforced concrete construction and the seams of mortar that hold them together. Triangles, circles and squares appear to have been punched out of the building's external walls as if by a giant cookie cutter. While they fit with the modern feel of the building, they are in fact a nod to the patterns used in traditional Bengali handicrafts, such as *jamdani* textile weaving. Within, the feeling is less brutal and more refined. The geometric windows allow for light to flood in and play on the white marble that clads the interior walls, and hallways lead into a domed amphitheatre where the country's parliamentarians gather.

The building also nods to the country's Islamic heritage. The site is oriented west, towards Mecca, and a prayer hall sits in the south of the complex. It's a reminder that this is far more than a civic space; it's also a monument to the spirit, freedom and resilience that lie at the heart of Bangladesh.

+ WHILE YOU'RE HERE

As both the capital and the largest city in Bangladesh, Dhaka is home to some of the country's finest architecture. Southeast of the National Assembly Building is the red-brick Curzon Hall, a university building that dates back to the British Raj and combines European gardens and ornate Mughal balconies. A 20-minute walk from Curzon Hall lies the Baitul Mukarram National Mosque. Built to resemble the Kaaba in Mecca, Bangladesh's minimalist national mosque is a huge square monolith set in a Mughal-style garden.

Angkor Wat, surrounded by a moat in the middle of the jungle

SIEM REAP • CAMBODIA

ANGKOR WAT

WHERE Preah Sihanouk Ave **TRANSPORT** Take a tuk-tuk to the site or hire a car from Siem Reap **INFORMATION** Open 5am–5:30pm daily; ticket required (angkorenterprise.gov.kh)

A symbol of Cambodia (spot it on the national flag), Angkor Wat is the country's most popular tourist attraction by far. Explore its vast courtyards and crumbling temples and you'll soon see that it more than lives up to the hype.

It's one of Asia's – heck, the world's – most iconic sights: a multi-level stone palace, topped with beautiful carved sandstone towers, surrounded by an ancient moat and hidden away in Cambodia's jungle. Massive on the one hand (it's the largest religious structure in the world), this historic temple is also decorated with tiny details – no stone has been left unembellished and you could take hours admiring just one small, stupefying section. While it was constructed almost 1,000 years ago (and some sections have been overrun by nature), it's still in remarkable condition today.

A KHMER CREATION

Angkor Wat was built in the 12th century by King Suryavarman II in the sprawling imperial capital of the Khmer Empire (then known as Yaśodharapura, later known as Angkor). It was constructed as a state temple (*wat*), though some believe it was also intended as a grand funerary monument for the king. It wouldn't be surprising if it was both: the Khmers flourished from about 800 to 1400 CE, ruled by Hindu monarchs who considered themselves "god-kings" – and who built on an appropriately grand scale. Hinduism had spread to Southeast Asia around the 6th century CE via trade with India, but not long after Angkor Wat was completed the royal Khmer family converted to Buddhism, and the original Hindu temple gradually transformed into a Buddhist temple. In subsequent centuries, the *wat* and the surrounding city fell into disuse and were largely abandoned as the Khmer capital moved to Phnom Penh. When the French colonized Cambodia in the 19th century, the site was rediscovered and excavated, but wars well into the 20th century took a heavy toll, and it was only from the

Clockwise from left
Ta Prohm Temple (better known as the Tomb Raider temple); young monks exploring the site; a giant Buddha sculpture

1990s – as a UNESCO World Heritage Site – that Angkor received the sensitive restoration it needed. Today, it's technically the most perfect example of medieval Khmer architecture in the world.

SACRED ARCHITECTURE

Angkor Wat was originally dedicated to Hindu deity Vishnu, and its layout reflects the Hindu mandala (sacred design of the Hindu cosmos). Its 3.6-km (2.2-mile) outer walls symbolize mountain ranges, its moat stands in for the ocean, and its five lotus bud-shaped towers represent Mount Meru, the five-peaked home of the *devas* (Hindu deities). Within the temple, there are three rectangular sandstone galleries stacked on top of each other. It's worth taking extra time over the bas-reliefs that line the walls of the outer gallery. You'll spot a host of historical and mythological figures: carved horses, elephants, bulls, lions and rhinos, along with the monkey god Hanuman, the serpent Vasuki and *garudas* (bird-like deities). There's also a section dedicated to the 32 hells and 37 heavens of Hinduism, with those in hell receiving grisly punishments and those in heaven uplifted by magnificent *garudas*.

A LOST CITY

While Angkor Wat is vast, it's nothing compared to the entire Angkor site. This long-abandoned city features more than 70 temples scattered across a vast plain that covers some 1,000 sq km (390 sq miles) – that's just a bit smaller than Los Angeles. It took an estimated five million tons of sandstone, 300,000 labourers and 1,000 elephants 30 years to build this lavish capital, and while it's all in ruins today, it's still an awe-inspiring site. It'd take days to cover the area on foot, so you'll need to hire a bike or a tuk-tuk driver to explore. And explore you must.

Perhaps second only to Angkor Wat is the temple of Ta Prohm, also known as the *Tomb Raider* temple after the 2001 film starring Angelina Jolie was shot here. It's one of the area's most atmospheric temples, its crumbling walls buckling under the weight of mammoth silk-cotton trees. Another highlight is the pyramid-shaped Bayon Temple, which features 54 towers bearing more than 200 huge stone faces. Both are must-sees, but Angkor Wat still rises above as the apex of Khmer architecture. There's a reason this masterful temple is on the Cambodian flag.

MORE LIKE THIS

Ayutthaya Historical Park, Thailand
This ancient city was founded in 1351 by Thai King Ramathibodi I, though the Khmers are thought to have built here much earlier.

Sukhothai Historical Park, Thailand
The remains of the capital of the Sukhothai Kingdom in the 13th and 14th centuries are a compact site with almost 200 palaces and temples.

Bagan, Myanmar
The ancient capital of the Burmese Pagan kingdom is now a vast ruin with some 2,200 Buddhist temples, pagodas and monasteries.

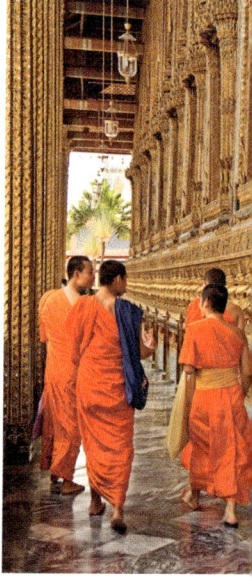

Clockwise from left Monks in Wat Phra Kaew; the palace's easy-to-spot spires; the palace's tiered roofs and plethora of gold design

63

BANGKOK · THAILAND

GRAND PALACE

WHERE Phra Borom Maha Ratchawang, Phra Nakhon **TRANSPORT** Khao San Rd (bus), Tha Chang (ferry), Saphan Taksin (Skytrain), Sanam Chai (MRT) **INFORMATION** Open 8:30am–4:30pm daily; buy tickets online or at the gate (royalgrandpalace.th)

Stately courtyards, royal residences, glittering Buddha statues – there's no greater monument to the gilded splendour of Thai history than the Grand Palace, a magnificent walled city in the heart of Bangkok.

Gaze across the Bangkok skyline and you'll see a bustling modern city dotted with skyscrapers. But wait, what's that? Dwarfed by glassy giants, a little legion of gilded spires, sloping pavilion roofs and soaring temple towers glitters in the sun. It's fairytale-esque and completely at odds with the rest of the city, but it's real.

This gleaming golden city is Bangkok's historic Grand Palace, a royal complex consisting of more than 100 buildings. It was built by King Rama I when he established the new Thai capital in Bangkok in 1782, and it's stood since then as a powerful symbol of the country's ruling royals – despite none of them having lived here since the 20th century.

Every inch of this city within a city is a work of art, but there are some unmissable highlights. Firstly, Dusit Maha Prasat. This extravagant throne hall features a four-tiered roof with a sumptuously decorated spire, plus a huge teak throne inlaid with mother-of-pearl. It's gorgeous, but there's more. For many, the Grand Palace's holy of holies is Wat Phra Kaew, the Temple of the Emerald Buddha and the most sacred Buddhist temple in Thailand. Built in 1785, it's adorned with gilded carvings of gods and mythical animals; within, every surface is decorated with murals from Buddhist mythology. As your eyes adjust to the half-light, though, they'll be drawn to one thing only: the Emerald Buddha itself, a statue carved from green semi-precious stone and hung with golden sashes, robes and bracelets, which shine in the candlelight. Now that's grand.

WHEN TO GO

The Emerald Buddha changes his outfit according to the time of year. In the rainy season, he wears a monk's robe over one shoulder, in summer he wears a sash and in winter he wears a cosy golden coat.

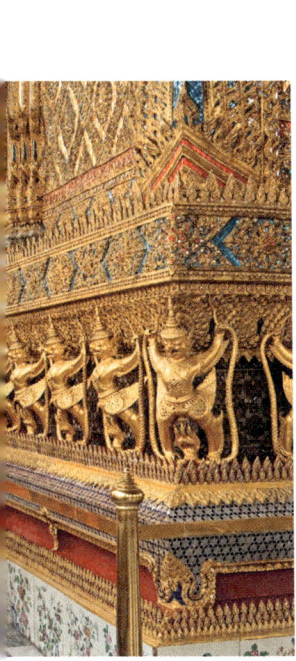

The gleaming towers, linked by a sky-high bridge

KUALA LUMPUR • MALAYSIA

PETRONAS TOWERS

WHERE Petronas Twin Towers, Kuala Lumpur City Centre **TRANSPORT** Ampang Park (metro) is the nearest stop **INFORMATION** Open 9am–9pm Tue–Sun; buy tickets online to avoid long queues (petronastwintowers.com.my)

The world's tallest twin towers loom like gleaming guardians over downtown Kuala Lumpur. Resembling two silver rockets, they're an apt symbol of the boom time that Malaysia – and Southeast Asia in general – has enjoyed.

All of contemporary Malaysia is embodied in the glittering twin spires of the Petronas Towers. The headquarters of state-owned petrochemicals giant Petronas, these lofty skyscrapers were built as a symbol of thriving modern Malaysia, all shining glass and steel. Yet traditional Islamic features (reflecting the country's spiritual heart) are represented in their design, too. The towers resemble mosque minarets, and their floor plan is based on the Rub el Hizb – an Islamic geometric pattern formed from two overlapping squares.

Completed in 1999, the Petronas Towers stand at 452 m (1,483 ft) and were the world's tallest building until they were usurped in 2004 by Taiwan's Taipei 101, which was then surpassed by Dubai's Burj Khalifa *(p108)*. Today, they're not even the tallest building in Kuala Lumpur – that honour goes to the Merdeka 118 skyscraper – but they remain the most iconic.

Stand at their feet and crane your neck skyward and their sheer scale is awe-inducing – particularly at night, when they're lit up and emit a ghostly glow against the velvet black sky. The real fun begins, though, when you step inside. With a full-size shopping mall, aquarium and science museum in the complex at the base of the towers (the Suria KLCC), you can make a full day of it here. There's even a concert hall, the Dewan Filharmonik, which hosts the Malaysian Philharmonic.

But first, you'll want to see the view. Tours lead visitors to the Skybridge, which connects the two towers on their 41st and 42nd floors and is the highest two-storey bridge in the world. From there, you'll ascend to the 86th-floor observation deck, from where you'll have even more spectacular views, including of the opposite tower. It is, after all, the highlight of the Kuala Lumpur skyline.

Right The hotel, home to 2,561 rooms

Below The infinity pool, Singapore's best viewpoint

SINGAPORE

MARINA BAY SANDS

WHERE 10 Bayfront Ave **TRANSPORT** Take the metro to Bayfront, then walk **INFORMATION** Tickets are required for the observation deck, open 10am–10pm daily (marinabaysands.com)

They don't make hotels like this every day. Home to a mall, two theatres, an ice-skating rink, celebrity chef-run restaurants and *that* famous infinity pool, this is a building you'll check into and never want to leave.

Slurping a bowl of noodles at a hawker centre, walking beneath the illuminated trees of the Gardens by the Bay, admiring the orchids of the Botanic Gardens – Singapore brims with iconic experiences. But ascending to the top of one of the world's most iconic hotels to sip on a sling while the sun sinks over the Lion City? That quite literally tops them all.

There aren't many hotels in the world that are immediately recognizable by their silhouette alone, but Marina Bay Sands became one of them when it opened in 2010. Its three towers are topped with the Sands SkyPark, a cantilevered platform that's been likened to a giant ironing board, a celestial surfboard and a bar of soap on stilts. Looks aside, it's what's inside (or on top) that matters most; up here you'll find tropical gardens, several bars and restaurants, and the world's largest infinity pool overlooking the skyscrapers and gardens of Singapore.

Leisure is at the heart of Marina Bay Sands, so it's fitting that architect Moshe Safdie's inspiration for the design was a deck of cards. There's something timeless about the blueprint, too, with the stacked construction of the towers and SkyPark resembling the megaliths and capstones of Stonehenge in the UK. But built as it was to be a talisman for Singapore's emergence as a global hub for business and tourism, the hotel is above all a modern, forward-thinking edifice. It's cutting-edge not just in its look but in its engineering; the three columns look straight from a distance but are actually slanted at 26 degrees, better to support the weight of the SkyPark.

In the evening, the Spectra Light and Water Show, which illuminates the plaza in front of the hotel, looks spectacular from the SkyPark's observation deck, with dancing jets of water lit up in purple, blue and green. It seems a shame, though, not to be able to enjoy a drink with the view, so forgo the ticket price for the observation deck and try to book a table at the exclusive Cé La Vi bar, clinging to a terrace beside the infinity pool. Cheers to that.

MORE LIKE THIS

Burj Al Arab, UAE
Another of the world's most eye-catching hotels is Burj Al Arab, which sits on its own artificial island and resembles a glass sail billowing from a mast.

Marqués de Riscal, Spain
Designed by legendary architect Frank Gehry, this luxury hotel features rumpled sheets of iridescent metal.

ASIA

+ **WHILE YOU'RE HERE**

The awe-inspiring Hindu temple complex of Prambanan lies around 45 km (28 miles) east of Borobudur and is another easy day trip from the nearby city of Yogyakarta. Built in the same period (9th century), Prambanan was dedicated to the "Trimūrti", the triad of Brahma, Vishnu and Shiva that together form the Hindu conception of the supreme being. The main site has a vast array of pointed stone towers and temples, second only in size to Cambodia's Angkor Wat (p152), with carvings and bas-reliefs considered masterpieces of classical Javanese art.

Left The massive tiered temple of Borobudur

Below One of the 72 smaller stupas on the temple

JAVA · INDONESIA

BOROBUDUR

WHERE Central Java **TRANSPORT** Buses to the site run from Yogyakarta or Semarang **INFORMATION** Open 9am–5pm Tue–Sun; book tickets online in advance (borobudur.injourneydestination.id)

It's been rocked by centuries of earthquakes and volcanic eruptions, and yet this gargantuan fortress of stone still stands tall above the Java plains. Meet Borobudur, the world's largest Buddhist temple.

What's a massive Buddhist temple doing in the heart of Indonesia, the world's biggest Muslim country? Looming above Central Java, Borobudur rises like a step pyramid, with nine platforms culminating in a giant stupa. Its existence reflects a time long before the arrival of Islam on the archipelago; it was likely built in the 8th and 9th centuries by the Sailendra dynasty, when Java was more influenced by the Hindu and Buddhist cultures of Gupta-era India. Abandoned, covered with volcanic ash and forgotten after most of Java converted to Islam in the 15th century, it was only excavated in the 19th century.

A BUDDHIST WORLD

Borobudur was built according to Buddhist principles, with the main structure's shape based on the mandala. Its nine stacked platforms of weathered, grey stone are also symbolic. The base represents the Buddhist concept of *kamadhatu*, the earthly realm; the 160 extraordinary reliefs here depict scenes of robbery, murder and torture, the consequences of earthly desires. The next five square terraces, embellished with stone carvings of Buddhist legends, represent *rupadhatu*, the transitional realm where humans are freed from these desires. The final three circular levels symbolize *arupadhatu*, the pure enlightened realm of the gods, and are free of ornament. Up here there are 72 smaller stupas, each containing a Buddha, though the giant stupa at the top is empty (it's not known why).

Indonesia may have changed since Borobudur was built, but folks still come here. You'll see them making a full 5-km (3-mile) circumambulation to the top, stopping to pray just as their forebears did over 1,000 years ago.

WHEN TO GO

To experience Borobudur at its most magical, visit during the Buddhist holiday of Vesak. It's usually held in May or June (during the full moon) and involves the release of thousands of floating "sky lanterns".

ASIA

OCEANIA

For many years, much of Oceania's architecture was inspired not by Oceania, but by the UK and the USA. Melbourne's Victorian centre mimicked the British Empire's style at the time, while the Sydney Harbour Bridge took the form of Hell Gate Bridge in New York. But then something changed. As nations began to acknowledge their past – and the Indigenous peoples who shaped it – buildings came to symbolize a move towards reconciliation. Take Australia's Bunjil Place, its design inspired by the creator deity of the local Indigenous peoples, or New Caledonia's Jean-Marie Tijbaou Cultural Centre, built to resemble the traditional homes of the native Kanak people. Many of the buildings here both look to the future and acknowledge the past, but there's fun to be had, too. Ever seen a cardboard cathedral?

PHOTO OPPORTUNITY

To capture the bridge and the Sydney Opera House in a single frame, take a seat on Mrs Macquarie's Chair in Sydney's Royal Botanic Garden. This historic sandstone bench has splendid harbour views.

Left *Walking on the roof of the bridge*

Below *The Sydney Harbour Bridge, spanning the northern and southern shores*

SYDNEY · AUSTRALIA

SYDNEY HARBOUR BRIDGE

WHERE 3 Cumberland St, The Rocks **TRANSPORT** Trains run to Sydney Central Station or take the bus, light rail or ferry to Circular Quay **INFORMATION** BridgeClimb tours take place 8am–8pm daily; ticket required (bridgeclimb.com)

Every city has a structure that reshapes its landscape forever, and for Sydney, it's this. Affectionately known as the "coat hanger" to Sydneysiders due to its arched design, the Sydney Harbour Bridge is an asset to the communities it connects.

This is one mighty engineering triumph, but don't just take our word for it – the numbers speak for themselves. It took 1,400 workers and 53,000 tonnes of steel to construct, covers an area equivalent to 60 football pitches and is crossed by over 150,000 vehicles every day. And it also happens to be the world's largest and widest steel arch bridge – mighty indeed.

STEELY DETERMINATION

Sydneysiders had nurtured an ambition to bridge their harbour since the early 1800s, but it wasn't until the 20th century that a proposal was put forward that would turn the idea into a reality. Having gathered design inspiration from Hell Gate Bridge in New York, chief engineer John Bradfield and his assistant Kathleen Butler hired a British steel-production and bridge-building firm, Dorman Long & Co, to tackle the construction. Using hand-driven rivets to connect over 550,000 pieces of steel, the team created the bridge's vast steel arch in two halves, making detailed calculations to ensure they met in the middle. At either end, close to the shore, massive hinges allowed expansion-related movement, and sturdy but non-structural stone towers added visual punctuation. When the bridge opened in 1932, it was an instant symbol of progress, innovation and modernity.

VIEW FROM THE BRIDGE

Visitors can walk, bike, drive or take the train across it, but arguably the best way to see the bridge is via the BridgeClimb, a 3.5-hour tour up ladders, catwalks and the upper arch. Firmly attached to a safety line, you'll be able to examine the steel structure up close while local guides share facts, such as how many rivets the bridge contains (over six million). From the top of the 134-m (440-ft) arch, the views of Sydney Harbour are unforgettable.

68

SYDNEY · AUSTRALIA

SYDNEY OPERA HOUSE

WHERE Bennelong Point **TRANSPORT** Trains run to Sydney Central Station or take the bus, light rail or ferry to Circular Quay **INFORMATION** Opening hours vary, check website (sydneyoperahouse.com); book a tour to see inside

One of the world's most recognizable buildings, the Sydney Opera House is an Aussie icon. And a building with a design as distinctive as this one can only have a whopper of a creation story to match.

When Danish architect Jørn Utzon won a competition to design Sydney's performing arts centre in 1956, he couldn't have imagined the legacy he'd leave. The staggered white shells of the building's famous roof have helped propel it, and Sydney itself, onto a thousand-and-one tourism brochures, which make its long, complicated birth utterly worthwhile.

When construction began in 1959, the plan was to complete it in four years to a budget of $7 million. In reality, it took an eye-watering $102 million and 14 years. The first issue? The site's geology hadn't been surveyed accurately and required huge concrete foundations that instantly strained the budget. Then there was Utzon's shell-shaped roof design, which worked on paper but was structurally unsound and far too heavy. But the roof made the design, and so Utzon began experimenting with shapes to see how it could come together. It's said that an epiphany came to him when he was peeling an orange: the curved roof shells could all come from a section of a sphere, with each piece precast in concrete and clad with clay roof tiles. He wouldn't stay on the project long enough to finish it, though; in 1966, demoralized by the government's reluctance to fund the spiralling costs, Utzon resigned, and Australian architect Peter Hall took over.

A CITY ICON

The Sydney Opera House finally opened its doors in 1973 and has been a modern icon ever since, even overcoming a few more building hiccups in the ensuing decades. But don't just stop at that famous exterior – enjoy the excellent programme of theatre, ballet and opera, or take a peek behind the curtain (and at the marvellous interiors) on a backstage tour. Considering the 11 million people it attracts a year, perhaps this building was worth the extra time and expense after all.

WHEN TO GO

The exterior might get all the attention, but the interior also has the wow factor, so book to see a performance – Opera Australia has a nine-month season from late July to April.

Clockwise from top
The iconic roof's chevrons, made up of 1,056,006 tiles; the Concert Hall; the roof, which self-cleans in the rain

OCEANIA 169

Clockwise from left The Princess Theatre; State Library; Royal Exhibition Building

MELBOURNE · AUSTRALIA

MELBOURNE'S VICTORIAN ARCHITECTURE

WHERE Throughout central Melbourne **TRANSPORT** The City Circle tram connects the city's major attractions and is free to ride **INFORMATION** Sites have specific opening hours, so check ahead (visitmelbourne.com)

Raised in post-Gold Rush opulence, central Melbourne's arrestingly ambitious Victorian buildings – running the gamut from theatres to stations to shopping precincts – are a highlight of any visit to this city.

In the 1850s, the huge wealth generated by the Victorian Gold Rush catapulted the state capital Melbourne into being the British Empire's second richest city. It was only right that it got a grand makeover to match. Today, the spread of what became known as Boom-Style buildings – ostentatious, ornamental late-19th-century affairs built by those who had got rich quick and wanted to show it – forms a characterful contrast with the city's gleaming late-20th- and 21st-century skyscrapers.

MUCH TO ADMIRE

How do you spot a Victorian building amid the city's contemporary constructions? It's all in the detail. Intricate mouldings, elaborate ornamentation, polychromatic brickwork and the use of cast and wrought iron are all tell-tale signs, many of which you'll spot from aboard the City Circle tram. Circling the city centre, with audio commentary along the way, this free heritage tram passes major Victorian landmarks: Parliament House, the State Library Victoria, the Princess Theatre and Flinders Street Station. Just beyond the tram's circuit is the pinnacle of Victorian sights: the Royal Exhibition Building, with a cast iron dome, high windows and an opulent interior.

It wasn't just public buildings that got the ornate treatment. Locals got in on the action, too, with houses featuring bay windows and balconies with filigree lacework. Many still stand today, so go house-hunting around inner suburbs like Fitzroy and Carlton; you'll be calling it "Marvellous Melbourne", just as the Victorians did, in no time.

MUST-SEE BUILDINGS

PARLIAMENT HOUSE
Raised in the mid-1850s, this building features plenty of finery, such as fluted columns, a floor mosaic and a wedding cake-like arcaded Queen's Hall *(Spring St)*.

STATE LIBRARY
The colonnaded State Library was built in Neo-Classical style in 1856. Its octagonal reading room with a soaring, domed ceiling was completed in 1913 *(328 Swanston St)*.

ROYAL EXHIBITION BUILDING
The city's only World Heritage-listed site is one of the few buildings left from the 19th-century world fairs *(9 Nicholson St, Carlton)*.

FLINDERS STREET STATION
The present station building, completed in 1910, features bright-yellow brickwork and an impressive bronze dome *(Swanston St/ Flinders St)*.

Right
The woven timber structure of Bunjil Place

Below *The building's light-filled foyer*

MELBOURNE · AUSTRALIA

BUNJIL PLACE

WHERE 2 Patrick NE Drive, Narre Warren **TRANSPORT** Narre Warren train station is within walking distance **INFORMATION** Box office, gallery and café opening hours vary, so check ahead (bunjilplace.com.au)

This isn't your average community hub. Rich in symbolism, Bunjil Place's impressive design represents the protection of the community and honours the area's original inhabitants.

When Bunjil Place opened in 2017, it was positioned as an inviting space for the community, one that celebrates belonging and civic pride. For the designers of the building, that didn't mean forgetting the community that came before – rather the opposite. The impressive design draws inspiration from the former occupier-owners of the land, the Boon Wurrung and Wurundjeri peoples of Victoria's Kulin nation, and the stories they told.

WHAT'S IN A NAME

For Victoria's Kulin nation, Bunjil is a creator deity in the form of an eagle, known for bringing the world into existence and protecting the land. But simply naming the centre after Bunjil wasn't enough. This depiction inspired the building's impressive roof, which unfurls in spectacular golden curves evoking spread-eagle wings. It's a seemingly weightless construction, supported at only two points on the floor, fluidly joining the interior's other functional spaces.

A COMMUNITY HUB

The inspiration didn't stop there. The designers also looked to Aboriginal artist Cathy Adams' 2001 painting *The Meeting of Many Paths*, which depicts indigenous wildlife journeying towards a central hub, a place where all are welcome. And that's exactly what Bunjil Place advocates. Underneath this roof, locals and visitors alike gather to experience ever-changing exhibitions, performances and film screenings, and to share ideas in the library and café. Community is at the heart of everything, as it's always been on this land.

MORE LIKE THIS

Setas de Sevilla, Spain
Known locally as "Las Setas" (The Mushrooms), this ultra-modern structure is formed of six wooden pavilions resembling *setas* (mushrooms), sheltering a market, museum and a sweeping walkway. The Observation Deck provides a soaring view of the city.

Pier Sixty, USA
Built within an original ship passenger terminal from 1911, events venue Pier Sixty is characterized by its huge, column-free interior and mighty floor-to-ceiling windows that let in big views of the Hudson River, in New York.

PERTH · AUSTRALIA

BELL TOWER

WHERE Barrack Sq, Riverside Dr **TRANSPORT** Bus or train to Elizabeth Quay, then walk **INFORMATION** Open 10am–4pm daily; ticket required (thebelltower.com.au)

This isn't just a building. Housing some of the rarest and most storied bells on the planet, Perth's Bell Tower is also one of the world's largest musical instruments.

At first glance, this is simply a spectacular modern building: a tapered glass structure adorned with two copper sails, representing regional sailing and metal-mining heritage. It's a surprise, then, to learn that this is actually a bell tower – something you expect to be part of a church or a civic building, not standing alone like this.

THE SOUND OF HISTORY

While the structure looks to the future, inside, the bells themselves mark time gone by. Of the now 18 bells inside the tower, 12 once belonged to London's St Martin-in-the-Fields church and date to at least the 14th century. They were first recast on the orders of Queen Elizabeth I and chimed upon the 1771 return of James Cook from his first voyage to Australia. In 1988, the British government gifted the bells to Western Australia to commemorate the country's bicentenary, making them the only set of royal bells known to have left England.

As well as looking pretty on Perth's skyline, the building is remarkable for its strength – it had to be reinforced with concrete cast in situ to bear the weight of the bells, today a whopping 9 tonnes. Aside from admiring the structure, the highlight, of course, is getting to hear the professional bell-ringers in action, so visit on a Thursday (midday–1pm) or Sunday (10:30–11:30am) for the ultimate musical treat.

Right The striking campanile, built in 1999

CHRISTCHURCH · NEW ZEALAND

CARDBOARD CATHEDRAL

WHERE 234 Hereford St **TRANSPORT** Buses run from central Christchurch to Hereford Street **INFORMATION** Open 9am–4pm Mon–Sat, 7:30am–5pm Sun (cardboardcathedral.org.nz)

Using a typically impermanent material – cardboard – to create a permanent and earthquake-proof building, the Cardboard Cathedral is the ultimate expression of how a city can bounce back from disaster better, brighter and more resistant.

Let's be frank: cardboard isn't a material that you'd think twice about using to construct a building. But Christchurch's Anglican Cathedral, built to replace the previous cathedral that was damaged in the 2011 Christchurch earthquake, shows that the material can be used to create impressive – and surprisingly permanent – structures.

AGAINST THE ODDS

Following the earthquake, Christchurch was in need of a temporary place of worship. The city called upon Japanese architect Shigeru Ban, a renowned "disaster architect" specializing in efficient, inexpensive buildings that provide short-term shelter for those impacted by natural disasters. Yet the building, which opened in 2013, proved such a potent symbol of new post-earthquake Christchurch life that it remains to this day.

So how do you build a cathedral out of cardboard? Well, the A-frame church is supported by some 98 cardboard tubes, each one waterproofed, fireproofed and reinforced with laminated wood. Shipping containers, meanwhile, help form the walls. Quirks in the structure don't stop there. The cathedral shies away from the traditional rose window, opting instead for 49 individual triangular panes of stained glass that make up the captivating main triangular window. Expected to last for 50 years, this building represents hope: for the city, its people and the future of architecture.

WHEN TO GO
Every Sunday at 5pm, and Tuesday through Thursday at 5:30pm (during school terms), the cathedral choir performs beautiful choral evensong. Check the website for details.

Next page The cathedral, which attracts 300,000 visitors annually

OCEANIA 175

Three of the giant huts, incorporating traditional and modern materials

NOUMÉA · NEW CALEDONIA

JEAN-MARIE TJIBAOU CULTURAL CENTRE

WHERE Rue des Accords de Matignon, Tina **TRANSPORT** Schedule a taxi to take you to and from the site **INFORMATION** Open 9am–5pm Tue–Sun; ticket required (centretjibaou.nc)

One of the planet's most arresting representations of Indigenous culture in architecture, this masterpiece is laid out to symbolize giant huts typical of the Kanak, a people tracing their roots back deep into New Caledonia's ancient past.

Cast adrift to Australia's northeast, the archipelago of New Caledonia is a French overseas territory, yet over 40 per cent of its inhabitants are Kanak, the original occupiers of this land. The Kanak have long spearheaded a movement to gain their home independence, and Jean-Marie Tjibaou, a tribal chief's son turned politician, became the main proponent of this fight in the 1980s. In 1988, Tjibaou signed a peace deal, ending a period of conflict between the Kanak and the Caldoches, pro-French inhabitants of New Caledonia. Because the deal postponed an independence vote for a decade, a radical Kanak activist viewed it as a betrayal, assassinating Tjibaou in 1989. This centre was commissioned in Tjibaou's honour.

CONNECTION TO CULTURE

New Caledonia, and thus the Kanak, never did gain independence – islanders voted against it in referendums between 2018 and 2021. But the Jean-Marie Tjibaou Cultural Centre at least serves to promote Kanak heritage and culture within New Caledonia. Designed by renowned architect Renzo Piano, it takes the form of ten "huts" inspired by traditional Kanak dwellings, with the taller structures within the complex representing the grander huts Kanak chiefs would have occupied. The design also takes inspiration from the Kanak people's strong connection to nature, and uses a mix of traditional Kanak building materials (wood, stone and coral) alongside aluminium, laminated wood and insect-resistant iroko wood from Africa.

Enveloped by lovingly landscaped gardens and surrounded by water, these huts might seem like large versions of centuries-old Kanak dwellings outside, but they're strikingly modern within and all serve a distinct purpose. Some house exhibition spaces and studios for music, dance or art; others a library and research rooms. However you explore the site, it's the perfect place to learn more about, and celebrate, Kanak culture.

WHEN TO GO

The centre hosts many events throughout the year, including open-air film screenings, dance and music festivals, artists-in-residence programmes and a women's market one Sunday a month, so check the events calendar on the website.

NORTH AMERICA

Skyscrapers, right? That's what North America is most famous for when it comes to architecture. It's where these super-tall structures originated, and today it's home to some of the most famous examples, like the Empire State Building, the Space Needle and the CN Tower. But North America's starchitects didn't always build up (and up and up) – just look at Frank Lloyd Wright's famously horizontal masterpieces. And actually, the buildings here aren't all modern. North America's architecture goes way back: Mesoamerican monuments, including incredible Mayan pyramids, have become icons of Mexico, while ancient Ancestral Puebloan settlements speak of a time long before the USA was even, officially, born.

NEW YORK CITY • USA

STATUE OF LIBERTY

WHERE Liberty Island **TRANSPORT** Ferries run from the Battery depot
INFORMATION Open 9am–5pm daily; ticket required to visit the crown (nps.gov)

She's New York's favourite leading lady. Rising above the waters of the Hudson, this iconic copper-clad statue has welcomed new New Yorkers for decades. Today, she remains a symbol of the city and the freedom it's long promised.

It's a bit of a stretch, but you could argue that the Statue of Liberty was New York's first skyscraper. After all, her internal structure is comprised of cast iron and stainless steel (like many modern skyscrapers) and her height (including the plinth she sits on) is equivalent to a 22-storey building. Back when she graced the Hudson horizon in 1886, she was the tallest building in the city – and to both locals and immigrants sailing past her en route to Ellis Island, her towering torch appeared to, quite literally, scrape the sky. That was over a hundred years ago, of course; today, she hardly reaches the knees of the city's glassy giants.

MOTHER OF FREEDOM

The best way to see the Statue of Liberty is from the water, and luckily that's how everyone has to arrive at Liberty Island, where she has stood since 1886. Celebrated French sculptor Frédéric Auguste Bartholdi fashioned her so she would have maximum effect when viewed from an ocean liner or boat; architect Richard Hunt built a multi-stepped plinth for her to stand upon (a small building in itself); and engineer Gustave Eiffel fashioned a steel armature for her that could endure the strongest winds. But who paid for the copper-clad Green Goddess? French citizens, in fact, who threw in their (then) francs for a statue to honour French–American bonds, and to acknowledge a brand of democracy forged in America and later exported.

She's iconic from afar, but her title gains more meaning up close. Liberty Enlightening the World (to give her her official name) carries a torch (symbolizing progress), wears a seven-pointed crown (akin to a halo, and into which you can climb), holds a book (etched with the date of the Declaration of Independence) and stands on a broken chain (symbolizing the abolition of slavery). She hovers above the waters leading to the Atlantic, marking the geographical start of Manhattan and the metaphorical entrance to American democracy. Spot Lady Liberty and you know you're now in the land of the free.

The Statue of Liberty, atop a 27-m- (89-ft-) tall pedestal

+ **WHILE YOU'RE HERE**

Didn't manage to view Lady Liberty up close? Head into the city to see an exact replica of her instead. Standing in front of an office building at 667 Madison Avenue is a bronze version of the otherwise copper-clad woman, made from the original plaster cast. This diminutive copy of Liberty may stand just 2.7 m (8.9 ft) tall – which is about 1/16th the size of her fully realized version – but she still gives a unique opportunity to see the details of the statue up close.

The Empire State Building, now New York's eighth tallest skyscraper

NEW YORK CITY • USA

EMPIRE STATE BUILDING

WHERE 350 Fifth Ave, between 34th and 33rd Sts **TRANSPORT** The nearest subway stations are 33rd St and Park Ave, or 34th St **INFORMATION** Open 9am–12am daily; ticket required (esbnyc.com)

It's the world's most photographed building, and one of the most visited. It's so vast that it has its own ZIP code. It's an Art Deco beauty and New York's original architectural icon. It's obviously the Empire State Building.

Few buildings have featured in as many films and TV shows as the Empire State. Whether it's the star of a sweeping New York City shot (think *Gossip Girl* or *Sex and the City*) or a plot point in itself (King Kong famously clung to its tip and Buddy the Elf worked inside), this Art Deco icon has become one of the world's most recognizable buildings. It's also among the first sights any visitor to New York wants to see, and may see sooner than they expect: most spot it when travelling into Manhattan from one of the city's airports. While it fights for elbow room among an ever-growing forest of skyscrapers and has fierce competition for height – One World Trade Center comes in at 541 m (1,775 ft), while the Empire State reaches 381 m (1,250 ft), though its TV tower extends it to 443 m (1,453 ft) – it still prevails on the midtown skyline as the fairest of them all.

BUILDING AN ICON

Before the Empire State Building commanded the New York skyline, another beauty stood in its place: the Waldorf Astoria Hotel. During the Gilded Age, this opulent hotel was the destination of the day for New York's upper crust, who sipped on sparkling wine and socialized in its extravagant rooms. But as fashions and fortunes changed, the hotel was sold and dismantled, and its elite corner spot became the base for another storied structure.

Construction of the Empire State Building began in 1929 (fortunately, financing had been secured prior to the stock market crash) and lasted a mere 14 months from foundation to final rivet. That's no small feat for what would become America's tallest building (temporarily, at least). But it wasn't rising alone. The "Race to the Sky", as the newspapers dubbed it, had begun, and New York quickly became a battlefield for soon-to-be skyscrapers. Early designs for the Empire State called for a shorter 50-storey building, but as rivals like the Chrysler Building climbed higher, the pressure to win the race mounted. And so, 50 storeys became 60, which became 80 and then finally 102. The "Race to the Sky" had a winner.

THE FINAL DESIGN

The Empire State Building didn't just become famous because it was tall. This limestone tower has a stately beauty to it as it rises from street level, gradually recessing in portions and culminating in a telescoping tower. Its main shaft is surprisingly bare, but there are subtle visual effects here: all 6,400 windows are set slightly out from the façade, and each storey is demarcated by aluminium spandrels. It's neat, elegant and very Art Deco.

But have you seen it at night? As the sun sets, the Empire State's sandy façade is bathed in an array of colours, depending on the holiday or notable anniversary (for instance, the birthday of Frank Sinatra, "Ol' Blue Eyes", sees the building bathed in blue). Gaze up at the very top and you'll see another light show: flashing visitors' cameras appear like shooting stars on the observation decks.

There's more drama inside. The main entrance on Fifth Avenue is an exhilarating (and echoing) three-storey-high space, with walls clad in red-and-grey marble and gleaming murals. The two side entrances (on 33rd and 34th Streets) are a little less dramatic: just two storeys in height, with corridors crossed by aluminium bridges. Sixty-two elevators (once all manually operated) service the floors, with some reserved for a non-stop ride to the dizzying heights of the observation decks.

TOP-FLIGHT

Nothing quite prepares you for the view at the top of the Empire State Building. Looming over central Manhattan, the skyscraper provides jaw-dropping views of the city below – there's the green rectangle of Central Park, the Statue of Liberty *(p182)* and the hazy Atlantic in the distance. Yet there's more than meets the eye here. In keeping with the building's intended role as the most modern building of all, its top storey was actually designed to serve as a docking point for blimps, then a promising form of air travel. The station (of sorts) served its purpose only twice: once in 1931, when a private dirigible spent three minutes up there, and again two weeks later when a Goodyear blimp made a fast delivery before floating off.

Times have changed, and so have skyscrapers. With the advent of all-glass façades in the 1960s, a new era of building was born; yet the Empire State Building has never lost its allure. Even New Yorkers well used to seeing it can't resist looking up... and up... and up at the city's original (and arguably best) skyscraper.

PHOTO OPPORTUNITY

Although the Empire State Building is always ready for its close up, it's even more dazzling when its full profile is captured from afar. For the best view, you'll need to climb another skyscraper, the Rockefeller Center; the Top of the Rock observation deck offers unobstructed views.

Clockwise from right
The Empire State's observation deck; the dazzling lobby; the view from the Top of the Rock; Art Deco signage

NORTH AMERICA 187

NEW YORK CITY · USA

GUGGENHEIM MUSEUM

WHERE 1071 Fifth Ave, between 88th and 89th Sts, New York City **TRANSPORT** Lexington Avenue and 86th St is the nearest station (ride the 4, 5 or 6 train) **INFORMATION** Open 10:30am–5:30pm daily; buy tickets at the gallery or online (guggenheim.org)

There are lots of beautiful art galleries around the world, but few have buildings more famous than the art inside. New York City's Solomon R Guggenheim Museum is one of the few that do.

Conceived by acclaimed American architect Frank Lloyd Wright, this stark-white, spiralling structure touched down on Fifth Avenue in 1959 and has been home to world-class modern art ever since. The collection features over 1,900 artworks by 625 artists, but many visitors simply come to stare at the building's exterior. In a city of right angles, these giant, stacked semicircles come as a thrilling surprise.

STARCHITECT AT WORK

Is this really the work of Frank Lloyd Wright?, you might ask as you look at the curves of the Guggenheim. For a man most famous for his long rectangular residences *(p195)*, this sinuous design looks a little left field. But Wright was always interested in organic forms, and a closer look reveals all the trademarks of America's most famous architect.

Cast in white concrete, this Modernist masterpiece features five storeys that not only coil upwards but also billow outwards, so that the top storey is the largest of all. Like many of Wright's buildings, its entryway is decidedly small, even cramped – though this was likely a deliberate design act to further heighten the dramatic interior. Pass through the doors, however, and you immediately come into one of the city's, indeed America's, most distinctive public spaces: a soaring atrium topped by an elaborately articulated glass skylight. The levels move upwards in exhilarating fashion, with artworks hung all along the walls. While tracing the spiral, you can see your fellow visitors over the parapet (which angles outward), and watching them ascend or descend is its own work of kinetic art.

After considerable architectural debate, the museum added a much-needed nine-storey rectangular addition in 1992 (by architects Gwathmey Siegel) that rises discreetly near the 89th Street side. Yet neither that building block nor any other nearby urban distraction interferes with the Modernist wonder of this building. Wright (a man never known for his modesty) is quoted as saying he created a "reposeful place in which paintings could be seen to better advantage than they have ever been seen". While that claim is debatable, there may be no other place more memorable to see artwork than this.

Left The curvaceous exterior of the Guggenheim

Below The coiling interior ramp, linking the galleries

MORE LIKE THIS

Gilder Center for Science, Education and Innovation, USA
Part of the American Museum of Natural History, this exhibition centre was designed by American architect Jeanne Gang. It takes the form of a warren of caves, seemingly carved out of a mountain in the middle of NYC.

Fondation Louis Vuitton, France
A Deconstructivist masterpiece, this art museum and cultural centre was designed by Frank Gehry and hosts a collection of modern art.

The US Capitol, a Neo-Classical landmark

77

WASHINGTON, DC · USA

NEO-CLASSICAL WASHINGTON

WHERE Central DC (US Capitol Visitor Center is First St at E Capitol St) **TRANSPORT** Most buildings are within walking distance of one another; the city also has a metro service **INFORMATION** Hours vary, check individual buildings; Capitol Visitor Center: 8:30am–4:30pm Mon–Sat (visitthecapitol.gov)

The White House, Capitol, Supreme Court, Lincoln Memorial – Washington, DC is crammed with architectural eye candy. The capital of the USA since 1790, it's a city designed to impress, with a dazzling Neo-Classical style that reflects the ideals of the founders.

Walking down the neat, wide boulevards of Washington, DC you might wonder, where are all the skyscrapers? After all, this is the capital of the USA, a country famed for inventing these lofty towers and building them in most major cities. Washington, DC, however, is a little different. Here, the streets are dominated by stately, white-stone buildings, with majestic porticos, symmetrical columns and decorative domes. And they're all in one particular architectural style: Neo-Classical.

WHY NEO-CLASSICAL?

America declared its independence from Great Britain in 1776, and in 1789 elected George Washington as the nation's first president. A year later, the country's founding fathers decided on a capital for their new nation. The decision came down to a now-famous compromise: in return for agreeing to Alexander Hamilton's plan for the government to take on the states' Revolutionary War debts, Thomas Jefferson and James Madison secured the federal capital on territory bridging the northern and southern states. A deadline of 1800 was set to transform this swampy land along the Potomac River into a place fit for the government of a new nation. French-born engineer Pierre Charles L'Enfant was selected to design the city in 1791, and though he was fired a year later by Washington (for insubordination – L'Enfant seemed to upset everybody he worked with), his grid plan for the city survived, along with the basic outline of two buildings: the White House and the Capitol.

There was little debate about what the new capital would look like. From the start, the city's architects leaned towards the Neo-Classical style, partly in response to its popularity in Europe (revivals of ancient Greek and Roman architecture dominated the 18th and 19th centuries, a reaction against Baroque, which was considered too showy). But Neo-Classical architecture wasn't just trendy. As leaders of a newly independent

republic, the founding fathers were also attracted to the movement's epic history. Neo-Classical revived the ancient Greek designs used for temples and grand public buildings, and the USA aspired to the democratic spirit pioneered by the city states of Greece. They built like them to be like them.

BUILDINGS FIT FOR A CAPITAL

With such an ambitious deadline (10 years to build an entire city was no easy feat), work began immediately. First up was the Capitol. Home of the legislative branch, this was deemed the most important building and was designed by amateur architect William Thornton, who was inspired by Greek Revival buildings in France. At the same time, Irish-American architect James Hoban designed the "President's Palace" (now the White House), modelling it on the Palladian-style Leinster House of his home town, Dublin. Both buildings were partly complete by 1800, technically making the deadline (though the Capitol was modified several times in the 19th century as Congress expanded with the nation). Today, the Capitol remains DC's most iconic building, a temple of democracy that dominates the National Mall – you can see its dome from just about anywhere in the city – and looks even grander up close, like a massive cathedral. But what's inside? Take a guided tour of the lavish interior to gaze upon smooth marble surfaces and world-famous art – Italian-American artist Constantino Brumidi's painting *Apotheosis of George Washington* on the inside of the dome is especially stunning.

Want to see Congress in session? You'll need to book a separate ticket to access the galleries.

It's much harder to tour the White House (spaces are limited), but the mansion can be seen through the iron fences surrounding it. A simple two-storey Georgian house, it's less lavish than the Capitol (this is a home, after all) but equally elegant, with a distinctive temple-like North Portico and landscaped front lawn.

... AND A SUPERPOWER

It was a good start, but it wasn't until the early 1920s that plans were approved for more government buildings and monuments. After a century or so, you might expect the architectural style to have changed. It hadn't. Most of these new buildings were constructed in the Neo-Classical design, too.

And so came more iconic monuments. The Lincoln Memorial arrived in 1922. An almost sanctimonious place (visitors instinctively lower their voices), it features a grand staircase, 36 fluted Doric columns and a giant statue of the 16th president – America's other presidents may have been a little jealous. A few years later, the Supreme Court opened. Resembling a Greco-Roman temple, the building is flanked by allegorical statues and topped by a massive Corinthian portico of white marble – walk up the stairs and you'll feel very small. By the 1940s, the city centre was packed with grand buildings (from memorials to government houses to museums) that dwarfed the White House; like Rome itself, the USA had come a long way, from nascent republic to global superpower.

Clockwise from left
The Lincoln Memorial, with 36 columns (one for each state at the time of his death); the Apotheosis of George Washington *on the Capitol dome; the grand Supreme Court*

MUST-SEE BUILDINGS

US CAPITOL
Every year, around 4 million people visit this breathtaking building *(1st & East Capitol Sts)*.

WHITE HOUSE
Every president except George Washington has called this Neo-Classical mansion home *(1600 Pennsylvania Ave NW)*.

LINCOLN MEMORIAL
Looming over the Reflecting Pool, this iconic memorial features a huge, seated figure of Lincoln *(Constitution Ave)*.

US SUPREME COURT
This elegant Corinthian building opened in 1935 *(1st St)*.

SAAM AND NPG
The Smithsonian American Art Museum (SAAM) and the National Portrait Gallery (NPG) share space in a huge Neo-Classical building *(8th & F Sts NW)*.

NATIONAL ARCHIVES
Want to see the original Declaration of Independence? Head to this boxy Neo-Classical beauty *(Constitution Ave)*.

78

ST LOUIS · USA

GATEWAY ARCH

WHERE 11 N 4th St **TRANSPORT** It's a short walk from the 8th & Pine or Laclede's Landing stations **INFORMATION** Open 9am–6pm daily; ticket required for tram (gatewayarch.com)

True, it's technically the world's tallest arch, but this isn't just an arch – there's a small tram inside, an observation deck on top and a surrounding national park.

Soaring above the Mississippi like a silver rainbow, the Gateway Arch was built to celebrate Thomas Jefferson's purchase of the vast Louisiana Territory in 1803, which doubled the size of the USA (part of the area was later renamed the Missouri Territory). The idea came about in the midst of the Depression years – a new memorial had the potential to revive St Louis' riverfront and create thousands of jobs. However, funding and planning delays meant that the winning design (by Finnish-born architect Eero Saarinen) wasn't completed until 1965. It's now part of the Gateway Arch National Park (the smallest national park in the USA), which includes the arch, its museum and the nearby Old Courthouse.

A glittering arc of steel, the Gateway Arch's immense size is hard to appreciate until you get up close – it's a whopping 192-m (630-ft)-tall hoop, seemingly sculpted by giants. In fact, it's made of a series of prefabricated triangles, narrowing as they approach the summit and hoisted into place by a crew of cranes and derricks that rose with the structure – the construction was so extraordinary that a viewing tower was created for spectators to watch. The arch is actually hollow inside, in order to carry a specially designed tram up to an observation deck on top (the four-minute ride is a bit like being on a Ferris wheel). From the top, the skyscrapers of St Louis seem tiny by comparison, with views tracing the Mississippi and far across the Great Plains – the land Jefferson purchased all those years ago.

Right The Gateway Arch, located at the site of the founding of St Louis

MILL RUN • USA

FALLINGWATER

WHERE 1491 Mill Run Rd **TRANSPORT** It's easiest to drive: take Pennsylvania Route 381; the house is 30 km (20 miles) south of Exit 91 on I-76 **INFORMATION** Open 8am–4pm Thu–Tue; ticket and tour required (fallingwater.org)

When Frank Lloyd Wright designed this private residence in 1936, he sought not only to embrace nature but to defy it. He accomplished both goals, creating perhaps the most famous house in America.

The clue is in the name. Perched precariously over a rushing waterfall, Fallingwater is the kind of house that stops you in your tracks: it's huge, with soaring stone chimneys and a series of broad terraces cantilevered over the falls. Yet somehow it doesn't feel out of place in a nature reserve in Pennsylvania. That's because Frank Lloyd Wright's masterpiece is a perfect example of organic architecture: the house doesn't simply sit on its environment, it's embedded in it. As the famed American architect once said: "The site and the house are one." And he was right.

Walk out onto the terrace and you'll hear the water and feel the mist. Venture inside and you'll bask in natural light flitting through large windows (which act as frames for the forest beyond). Tour guides at the house will also point out that the materials here are mostly local (stone, like the waterfall's foundations, and sandstone, quarried locally). It's clear that Wright loved the surrounding landscape, and he wasn't the only one.

Fallingwater was built in the 1930s for the local Kaufmann family, who commissioned Wright to build a weekend retreat near the waterfall they loved; he one-upped them and built a house *on top* of the falls. The Kaufmanns moved out decades ago, but Fallingwater remains for all to enjoy – though be prepared for some serious house envy.

WHEN TO GO

The Fallingwater Institute (which hosts events at both the house and related locales) offers year-round classes and lectures about the residence. Sign up, perhaps, for a plein air painting session in the house, or a writing course that uses the house as inspiration.

Next page *Fallingwater, cocooned in the Pennsylvanian landscape*

CHICAGO · USA

THE CHICAGO SCHOOL

WHERE The best examples are found in the "Loop", Chicago's main downtown area
TRANSPORT These are all walkable streets, though you might want to rent a city bike and pedal the route, especially on weekends, when there is less traffic

Think New York is skyscraper central? Think again. Decades before the Empire State Building reached for the sky, architects in Chicago were laying the building blocks for their own super-tall structures, many of which can still be seen today.

For generations, architects and architectural historians graduated from the Chicago School, although there is no campus or headquarters housing it, nor is there any official curriculum. Rather, the Chicago School was an architectural phenomenon that emerged in the late 19th century and came to define Chicago for decades.

GOING TO SCHOOL
It all began in 1871, when the Great Chicago Fire swept through the city, destroying nearly everything in its path (it didn't help that many of the city's buildings were made of wood). The aftermath was devastating, but out of the ashes, a new era was born. Budding architects now had a blank canvas to build on, and, better yet, technological breakthroughs meant they had the tools to make something new. Thanks to advances in glass-making and revolutionary construction techniques – primarily, new steel superstructures (on which masonry could be easily assembled) – the sky became their only limit. Super-tall buildings (some up to 16 storeys) could now be built quickly, and consequently a slew of office towers began appearing in the city centre. Many of them featured distinctive "Chicago windows" – characterized by a large, fixed centrepiece of glass bracketed by double-hung sash windows on either side – alongside decorative scrolling and elaborate cornices. The result? Elegant buildings infused with natural light that just so happened to be America's first skyscrapers.

While Chicago, like other American cities in the 1960s, demolished many of its early skyscrapers in favour of modern ones (or car parks), the city still features some examples of Chicago School masterpieces. Many of these remain office buildings, while others have become sought-after apartments. You'll find the best examples in the city's central area, known as the "Loop". Take a walk around, pausing to crane your neck up at the lofty towers – look out for terracotta cladding (which many architects favoured during the Chicago School era), top floors capped with cornices and, of course, those classic Chicago windows. Don't be shy about walking into the lobbies for a closer look, too.

MUST-SEE BUILDINGS

MONADNOCK BUILDING
The Monadnock was the tallest office building in the world when completed in 1893; spot the large copper cornice of its roof *(54 W Van Buren St)*.

SULLIVAN CENTER
The former Carson Pirie Scott department store features the first known Chicago windows *(1 S State St)*.

RELIANCE BUILDING
A classic Chicago School structure, the Reliance Building features projecting bay windows and terracotta cladding *(32 N State St)*.

SECOND LEITER BUILDING
This is one of the earliest still-standing commercial buildings constructed with a metal skeleton frame in the USA *(403 S State St)*.

Clockwise from top
The terracotta-clad Reliance Building; Chicago windows on the Reliance Building; lifts inside the Reliance Building

81

SEATTLE · USA

SEATTLE CENTER

WHERE 305 Harrison St **TRANSPORT** The Seattle Center has a monorail station; the nearest bus stop is 5th Ave N & Broad St **INFORMATION** Open 7am–9pm daily; the grounds are free to enter (seattlecenter.com)

A warped art gallery resembling a smashed electric guitar. A sky-high monolith topped with a saucer that looks like it's about to take off for the heavens. No, you've not entered an alternate psychedelic universe. This is the Seattle Center.

An entertainment hub home to some of Seattle's finest museums and music venues, the Seattle Center also hosts the city's most remarkable architecture. Many of its kaleidoscopic buildings were created for the 1962 World's Fair, but the Seattle Center has been part of the Emerald City's story since the very beginning. Sitting on land bequeathed to the city in 1886 by its founder, David Denny, this complex of entertainment and education venues really began to take shape in 1928, with the building of the Seattle Civic Auditorium. Now known as McCaw Hall, this elegant site – understated compared to its neighbours – has long been a centre of arts; today, it's home to the Seattle Opera and Pacific Northwest Ballet.

It wasn't until the 1960s that things started to get a little weird. What started as a doodle on a place mat by Edward Carlson, organizer of the 1962 World's Fair, later became Seattle's internationally recognized landmark: the mighty Space Needle. This 184-m (604-ft) monolith resembles a flying saucer atop a tall tripod, with its observation deck and revolving bar providing soaring views over Seattle's downtown. Similarly eye-catching, and also built for the World's Fair, is the Pacific Science Center, which features exhibits on aerospace, ecology and prehistory, plus a courtyard that's home to a set of towering "space arches" – 30-m- (100-ft-) tall, snow-white structures that look like giant aliens. Flying saucers, aliens, needles that reach for the stars: it's not hard to guess what Americans had their sights set on in the 1960s.

Later additions to the Seattle Center only got more gloriously bonkers. MoPOP (Museum of Pop Culture) was designed by architect Frank Gehry in 2000 and comprises colourful bands of shimmering sheet metal. Gehry was inspired by Seattle music legends Jimi Hendrix and Kurt Cobain, both of whom had a penchant for smashing their instruments on stage – the image of a mangled guitar is said to have inspired the building's design. It's eye-catching, to say the least.

Clockwise from left The Space Needle, an icon of Seattle; the "space arches" at the Pacific Science Center; the city's monorail, passing MoPOP

NORTH AMERICA 201

SAN FRANCISCO • USA

GOLDEN GATE BRIDGE

WHERE San Francisco **TRANSPORT** Begin your visit at the Golden Gate Welcome Center (reachable via MUNI city bus 28) **INFORMATION** Open 9am–6pm daily; it's free to cross on foot or bike, but there's a toll to cross by car (goldengate.org)

Is this the world's most famous bridge? It might just be the most recognizable. Rising above the chilly waters of the Pacific Ocean and San Francisco Bay's blanket of fog, the red-orange Golden Gate Bridge is an icon of the city.

Sunset over the Golden Gate Bridge

You've seen it in films, on postcards, even on album covers, but nothing quite prepares you for seeing it in real life. Spanning the Golden Gate Strait (hence the name), this 2.7-km- (1.7-mile-) long, 27-m- (89-ft-) wide icon is buffeted by winds and waves and regularly clouded by fog. And yet still it prevails. It was once the world's longest suspension bridge – it was overtaken by New York's Verrazzano Bridge in 1964 – but despite losing a superlative, the Golden Gate Bridge has remained the most famous symbol of San Francisco.

GETTING SUSPENDED

Plans to span the deep, cold, current-ridden Bay of San Francisco (from the city to Marin County) date back to 1872, but it wasn't until 5 January 1933 that construction of the bridge began. This was at the height of the Great Depression (not a great to time to start building), but the funds were in place and the main architect, Irving F Morrow, was already committed. There was no going back.

For four years, the world watched as the two notched towers rose from the water and huge steel cables were gradually hung between them. On 27 May 1937, the bridge opened for pedestrians only, and an estimated 200,000 people walked across its length. The road opened the next day, when an official convoy of Cadillacs and Packards became the first vehicles to cross.

But what about the colour? Most folks think it's red, but technically the bridge is painted in "International Orange", a reddish-orange tint that matched the shade of the steel parts when they arrived from mills in New Jersey and Pennsylvania, all coated in a protective reddish primer. A version of that colour was replicated and has remained its permanent hue ever since. It was a good choice: despite the fogs that blight the bay, the bridge can always be seen through the mist. Plus, there aren't many red-orange bridges around the world; pair that with the scenic setting and it's no wonder photographers and filmmakers love it.

SAN SIMEON • USA

HEARST CASTLE

WHERE 750 Hearst Castle Rd **TRANSPORT** Closest Amtrak/Greyhound station at Paso Robles (64 km/40 miles east) **INFORMATION** Tours 9am–5pm daily; book tickets online (hearstcastle.org)

What's your dream home? For William Randolph Hearst it was a Spanish-inspired castle complex, sprawled across a section of California coast. Fortunately for him, he had the money to make his dreams a reality.

When architect Julia Morgan first met multi-millionaire W R Hearst in 1919, she was already a pioneer: the first woman to win entry to the prestigious École des Beaux-Arts in Paris, and the first female licensed architect in California. But Hearst would forever change her life: his castle was the commission of a literal lifetime and Morgan would work on it for near 30 years.

Born in 1863, the son of a multimillionaire, Hearst made his own fortune in magazine and newspaper publishing. He became an icon, loved and loathed in equal measure. Indeed, when Orson Welles's film *Citizen Kane* was released in 1941, loosely based on the media mogul, an incensed Hearst banned any mention of it in his newspapers. Needing a place to escape the media glare, store his vast art collection and entertain in privacy, Hearst chose an isolated piece of land on the Pacific Coast.

SPANISH BAROQUE FANTASY

The entire complex – which includes guest houses, outdoor pools and gardens – perches on a hill above the coast like a medieval Spanish city (Hearst loved the Renaissance and Baroque architecture of Spain). It was built in stages from 1922 to 1947, primarily in steel-reinforced concrete to withstand California's earthquakes. The main building, Casa Grande, is a Mediterranean Revival masterpiece, featuring two elegant bell towers modelled on a church in Ronda. It's just as sumptuous inside as out. Hearst pillaged medieval mansions, castles and monasteries in Europe to furnish the rooms with tapestries, manuscripts, oak tables and whole painted ceilings. The result is ostentatious to say the least, and, as in *Citizen Kane*, it really does seem to contain "enough for ten museums; the loot of the world".

PHOTO OPPORTUNITY

Sit on the right side of the shuttle bus from the visitor centre to the castle for the best views. Once there, the Neptune Pool is especially photogenic, as is the grand façade of Casa Grande (you can stand right out front to shoot it).

Clockwise from top
Sprawling Hearst Castle, akin to a Spanish town; a water fountain on the site; the Neptune Pool

Right The auditorium's stage, with its French fry-shaped organ

Below The exterior, made from 12,500 pieces of stainless steel

LOS ANGELES • USA

WALT DISNEY CONCERT HALL

WHERE 111 S Grand Ave **TRANSPORT** Grand Ave Arts/Bunker Hill is the nearest metro station **INFORMATION** Free self-guided audio tours are offered by the Music Center most days: 10am–3pm (no reservations required; last entry: 2pm)

An installation of gargantuan shells or a series of giant sails rippling in the wind? Regardless of how you interpret Frank Gehry's stainless-steel concert hall, it's still a dazzling place to see a show in.

Glittering in the LA sun, Frank Gehry's iconic Walt Disney Concert Hall is a mass of giant silver blocks and aerodynamic curves. It's distinctively Gehry, an almost chaotic array of shapes, or rather a masterclass in Deconstructivist architecture. But it was nearly very different: initial designs called for a stone building (hardly as dazzling); fortunately, following the success of Gehry's titanium-clad Guggenheim Museum in Bilbao *(p36)*, stone soon became steel – and it changed everything.

As you might expect from looking at the building, the construction process wasn't easy. Gehry's design of irregular curves was initially too complicated for contractors to understand. He resorted to using sophisticated software (normally used to design fighter jets) to get his vision across. But the project still took 16 years to build, and at one point some of the concave, stainless-steel panels had to be sanded so they wouldn't glare and cause traffic accidents (LA isn't short on sunshine, after all).

While the exterior is silvery and shell-like, the auditorium is more like a cosy cocoon, covered in head-to-toe hardwood. The organ (with pipes likened to French fries) and the wooden acoustical "clouds" that billow from the ceiling were designed by Gehry with advice from music experts, because this isn't just an architecturally perfect building, it's acoustically perfect, too. Settle in for a concert and you'll soon be surrounded by music and immediately immersed.

WHEN TO GO

There's always something going on in the hall, but Christmas is a particularly popular time to visit. Expect carols and themed shows galore.

MORE LIKE THIS

Jay Pritzker Pavilion, USA
The anchor of Chicago's Millennium Park since 2004, this open-air concert venue is another Frank Gehry classic, with a billowy "headdress" of brushed stainless-steel ribbons and an overhead trellis of steel pipes.

Weisman Art Museum, USA
Opening in 1993, this lesser-known Gehry masterpiece (an art gallery on the University of Minnesota campus) pre-dates Bilbao and LA but already showcases his innovative design, with an exterior of curving and angular steel sheets.

NORTH AMERICA

85

MESA VERDE NATIONAL PARK • USA

CLIFF PALACE, MESA VERDE

WHERE Cliff Palace Loop **TRANSPORT** The nearest city and transport hub is Cortez; from here, you'll need a car **INFORMATION** To enter all cliff dwellings you must have a reservation on a ranger-led tour; these run early May to late October (recreation.gov).

Venture deep into Colorado and you'll discover a lost city of stone. Tucked beneath a massive rock ledge, this cluster of sandstone walls, rounded towers and multistorey dwellings was once home to an Ancestral Puebloan civilization.

You can only drive so far. Perched halfway up a steep canyon wall in a dusty Colorado canyon, the ancient Cliff Palace isn't the easiest place to reach – and that's just how its ancient residents liked it. This remote (and easily defendable) site requires a rocky walk through the canyon, a clamber down uneven stone steps and a climb up four wooden ladders. En route, you'll only catch brief glimpses of the ruins through the pines and scrub, but when the path turns the final corner, there it is: a remarkable stone complex sprouting out of the cliff face, balanced some 30 m (100 ft) beneath a vast overhang. It's easily one of America's most impressive Pre-Columbian monuments.

A SANDSTONE MARVEL

Built between 1190 and 1280 CE by Ancestral Puebloans – a sophisticated civilization that flourished hundreds of years before the arrival of Europeans – the Cliff Palace was once home to over 100 people. Its vast complex features numerous multi-storey living spaces, plus 23 distinctive kivas with rounded towers that look like castle turrets (these are thought to have been ceremonial spaces). When outsiders first discovered the ruins in 1888, they were amazed by the level of engineering and artistic sophistication – somehow the builders were able to drag sandstone blocks and wooden beams up into the cave, then hold everything together with a natural mortar of soil, ash and water.

Mesa Verde was abandoned around 1300 for unknown reasons, but it remains a sacred space among Indigenous Americans. The Ancestral Pueblo people eventually migrated into what's now New Mexico and established historic pueblos where their descendants still live today – some of which are the oldest continuously inhabited communities in the USA.

Top The sprawling Cliff Palace, built into the rock face

Right Exploring the ruins of the Long House

MORE LIKE THIS

Chaco Culture National Historical Park, USA
The Chaco Canyon community thrived between 850 and 1250 CE, and these monumental Ancestral Puebloan ruins are evidence of the society's wealth. The site is set within a national park and includes highlights such as Chetro Ketl, a huge sandstone "great house", like an important ceremonial centre.

Taos Pueblo, USA
To see a spectacular example of where the descendants of the Ancestral Pueblo people live today visit this still-occupied pueblo, home of the Tiwa-speaking Taos Puebloan people. Set against a backdrop of the snow-tipped Taos Mountains, the town features a series of multi-storey, reddish-brown adobe residences, built between 1000 and 1450 CE.

Bright façades of Art Deco hotels lining the colourful Ocean Drive

MIAMI · USA

MIAMI ART DECO

WHERE Between 5th St and 23rd St, along Ocean Drive, Collins Ave and Washington Ave, South Beach, Miami Beach **TRANSPORT** The Miami Beach trolley and metrobus run to Washington Ave **INFORMATION** Guided tours are available (mdpl.org)

Whimsical, bold, fun and jaunty, Miami's Art Deco is an aesthetic you'll rarely see in other cities. You'll find more than 800 beautifully preserved buildings in the city's South Beach area, a designated Art Deco District.

Hip and glamorous, Miami's South Beach is known for its palm-backed sands and party scene, but behind the cocktails and convertibles lies an American treasure. Here you'll find the largest concentration of Art Deco architecture in the world: over 800 buildings from the 1930s and 1940s bedecked with geometric lines and curves, chrome and neon, spires and bold splashes of colour. And it's all thanks (mostly) to the work of preservationist Barbara Capitman, who created the Miami Art Deco District in 1979 to protect this great architectural legacy.

A SILVER LINING

Miami's Art Deco wonderland may not have existed if it wasn't for the destruction caused by the Great Miami Hurricane of 1926. The storm devastated the wooden buildings on Miami Beach in particular, and in subsequent years these were replaced with stronger concrete structures, with architects taking inspiration from a newly modish style emerging in Europe. Art Deco – combining Art Nouveau's sinuous lines and the geometric patterns of Cubism – made its debut at the 1925 Exposition Internationale des Arts Décoratifs et Industriels Modernes in Paris. The style proved a sensation, swiftly influencing a swathe of young architects in Europe and America, and particularly in Miami.

But why was it so popular? One answer is the Great Depression. Fun and whimsy were hard to come by in late-1920s America, so when buildings started popping up with quirky designs and playful decorations, the American population, you could say, saw a brighter future in them. And so Art Deco gem upon Art Deco gem appeared along Miami Beach (primarily along the streets in the region of South Beach).

TROPICAL DECO

Two principal styles began to dominate South Beach in the 1930s. The initial phase of more traditional Art Deco buildings was dubbed Tropical or Miami Deco. You'll see them all over South Beach, especially when strolling along the main thoroughfares, Ocean Drive and Collins and Washington Avenues. Many are hotels, and even if you're not a guest, you can go inside to check out the lobby or grab a drink at the bar. What makes them Tropical Deco? There are a number of distinguishing features: look for "eyebrows" above the windows, portholes, stepped rooflines and straight lines. In terms of embellishment, you'll spot reliefs featuring palm trees and flamingos and exotic designs inspired by ancient Egyptian, Aztec and African cultures. The Webster, at 1220 Collins Avenue, is a prime example. Designed by prolific architect Henry Hohauser, its straight-lined façade is embellished with beautiful friezes and carvings.

STREAMLINE MODERNE

Streamline Moderne is the style of Art Deco most associated with South Beach today; the buildings are sleeker, with hard edges rounded off. The Marlin Hotel, at 1200 Collins Avenue, is one of the finest examples, with rounded sides, a wonderfully decorative façade and a flagpole spire. It was designed in 1939 by L Murray Dixon, who along with Hohauser is primarily responsible for the district. Dixon also designed the Tiffany Hotel (now the Tony) at 801 Collins Avenue – its gorgeous terrazzo floors and mosaic mirrors have been faithfully restored, but its most iconic feature is the futuristic spire on top.

Want to learn more about Miami Art Deco? You'll get the best overview at the Art Deco Museum and Welcome Center (1001 Ocean Drive), which offers context on the style and its various iterations. The museum is run by the Miami Design Preservation League, and its thanks to this organization and the work of Barbara Capitman that Miami's buildings have a secure future. Yet, ironically, one of the signatures of Miami Art Deco was introduced by the league itself. It was Capitman's preservation partner, designer Leonard Horowitz, who came up with the now-beloved palette of bubblegum pinks, bright yellows and blues in the 1980s – originally, most Deco buildings were painted white. Would the district have become so famous if it had remained so plain? It certainly wouldn't feel so Miami.

WHEN TO GO

Architecture fans should consider visiting Miami during the annual Art Deco Weekend in January, which is organized by the Miami Design Preservation League. During this event, the area's architectural legacy is celebrated with live music, special walking tours and lectures.

Clockwise from right
The striking blue façade of the Breakwater; Ocean Drive's colourful ensemble of Art Deco; the lighthouse feature on Waldorf Towers

MUST-SEE BUILDINGS

CONGRESS HOTEL
This gorgeous example of Streamline Moderne by Henry Hohauser has a distinctive sign and "frozen fountains" framing the entrance *(1036 Ocean Dr).*

THE CAVALIER HOTEL
The Cavalier Hotel was designed by Roy F France in a Tropical Deco style, with sharp edges and a colourful exterior *(1320 Ocean Dr).*

WALDORF TOWERS
This cream-and-orange Art Deco hotel features an ornamental lighthouse on its roof *(860 Ocean Dr).*

THE BREAKWATER
Anton Skislewicz's Streamline Moderne building has racing stripes and neon signage *(940 Ocean Dr).*

THE AVALON
Designed by Albert Anis, this stripped-down Streamline building has an asymmetrical design and horizontal lines *(700 Ocean Dr).*

The fairytale-esque Château Frontenac in winter

87

QUÉBEC · CANADA

CHÂTEAU FRONTENAC

WHERE 1 Rue des Carrières   **TRANSPORT** The nearest bus stop is on Place d'Armes   **INFORMATION** Non-guests can visit the hotel's public areas and restaurants; guided tours (reservations required) are also available

No, you haven't stumbled into a Walt Disney film, but you could easily believe it. Welcome to Québec's most beloved building, a French fantasy castle complete with spires and towers, fit for a princess and her prince.

Once upon a time, there was a city in need of some TLC. Old Québec was founded long ago, in 1608, and by the late 19th century its cobbled streets and French colonial churches were starting to show their age. And so, a regeneration project was proposed, in order to create a more tourist-friendly destination. Its crowning jewel? A grand hotel conceived by William Van Horne, president of the Canadian Pacific Railway (a boom in well-heeled railway travellers required fittingly majestic lodgings) and designed by architect Bruce Price.

FRENCH MEDIEVAL FANTASY

Price knew he wanted something French in style, but the colonial architecture of Québec was too humble – he'd have to look further back in history for inspiration. What about French Baroque? Far too flamboyant. Or Neo-Classical? Too sober. How about French Renaissance? The architect finally found his template in the 14th- and 15th-century stone castles of France's Loire Valley. His gargantuan hotel melded Gothic and French Renaissance revival styles: though hung on a modern steel frame, the exterior was decorated like a Parisian wedding cake in red brick and stone, with wildly exaggerated spires, ornate gables and a steeply pitched copper roof. The interior was equally lavish, with enough marble, statuary and gilding to impress Louis XIV.

The project was a massive success: when it opened in 1893, Château Frontenac became a symbol for the romantic but wholly illusory view of Québec as a French medieval city. Indeed, Price's design became the archetype for a series of hotels built along the Canadian railways in a style known as "Châteauesque", after the Québec original. Today Fairmont Le Château Frontenac remains one of North America's most luxurious resorts, but only after having adapted once again, this time to attract discerning 21st-century travellers. The fantasy vibes remain, but now you'll be staying in the first historic hotel in Canada to achieve carbon neutrality.

88

TORONTO · CANADA

CN TOWER

WHERE 290 Bremner Blvd **TRANSPORT** Walk from Union Station **INFORMATION** Open 9am–9:30pm daily; buy tickets in advance (cntower.ca)

Mind-bendingly tall, the CN Tower looms over Toronto like a giant needle piercing the clouds. A wonder of modern engineering, it's a Canadian emblem as iconic as the maple leaf.

The closer you get to the CN Tower, the harder it is to comprehend its immense height – its sleek, narrow structure tapers like a minaret, so that from the base, it seems you could reach out and touch the top. You can't, of course – looming 553 m (1,814 ft) above Toronto city centre, the tallest free-standing structure in the Western Hemisphere dominates the skyline. Wherever you are in the city, look up and there it is.

The tower looks like a gargantuan TV mast, because it is: built in the 1970s, it remains a communications tower today, though tourism provides far more income. You'll get a better sense of its size once inside: riding its glass-fronted elevators to the top in under one minute remains a breathtaking experience. The Main Observation Level offers an epic 360-degree panorama of the surrounding pancake-flat prairies and Lake Ontario, Toronto itself reduced to a tiny model village (on a clear day you can even spot the mist of Niagara Falls). Thrill-seekers can also walk on a glass floor, or pay extra for the Edgewalk along the restaurant roof – it's a gut-wrenching 356 m (1,168 ft) high. More sedate pleasures beckon at 360 The Restaurant, which revolves slowly, offering sweeping views of the city as you eat. But really it's all about the elevation here: head to The Top (447 m/1,467 ft high), a confined little gallery that feels like it's really on top of the world, as will you.

Right The CN Tower, head and shoulders above Toronto's skyline

Next page
The massive Metropolitan Cathedral

MEXICO CITY · MEXICO

METROPOLITAN CATHEDRAL

WHERE Plaza de la Constitución **TRANSPORT** Zócalo/Tenochtitlan is the closest metro station **INFORMATION** Open 9am–6pm daily; the cathedral is free to visit (catedralmetropolitana.mx)

One of Latin America's largest churches wasn't built overnight. Constructed over centuries, this massive cathedral (more like a Spanish fortress) is a thrilling blend of architectural styles. Can you spot them all?

Stroll into the Zócalo (the plaza at the heart of old Mexico City) and you'll find yourself in the shadow of an icon. The great Metropolitan Cathedral dominates the area, rising 67 m (220 ft) high and featuring two towers, a shimmering dome and a wealth of ornamentation.

This staggering structure sits on the former site of the Aztec capital, Tenochtitlan (in fact, it was built by Spanish conquerors over the ruins of one of the biggest Aztec temples). Construction began in the 1520s, gradually extending over three centuries, and today it's a jumble of Spanish styles. Take time to admire the exterior: its elegant portals are Plateresque, while the hulking bell towers (rising 67 m/220 ft and containing 25 bells) are Neo-Classical additions. Best of all is the façade of the Sagrario Metropolitano to the right of the main entrance. An explosion of intricately carved details, it's a wonderful example of Spanish Churrigueresque of the late Baroque, a little slice of Madrid in Mexico.

Incredibly, under all of the cathedral's layers of stone, some Aztec remains have survived. In 1978, the ruins of an ancient temple (Templo Mayor) were accidentally discovered by an electrical company working near the cathedral. Centuries ago, they would've comprised the grandest structure in the Zócalo. Today, they are but a tiny piece of Tenochtitlan beneath the monolithic cathedral that rules the square.

PHOTO OPPORTUNITY

For the most sensational shot of the cathedral, you'll need to splash out on a meal (breakfast is the best deal) at the Terraza restaurant on top of the Gran Hotel de la Ciudad de México (granhoteldelaciudad demexico.com.mx).

NORTH AMERICA

Right Museo Soumaya, which some liken to the shape of a corset

Below The museum's sloping galleries

90

MEXICO CITY · MEXICO

MUSEO SOUMAYA

WHERE Blvd Miguel de Cervantes Saavedra **TRANSPORT** San Joaquín (metro) is the nearest station **INFORMATION** Open 10:30am–6:30pm daily; entry is free (museosoumaya.org)

The art inside the Museo Soumaya spans centuries (from ancient relics to modern sculptures), but the building is decidedly contemporary. A curving, contorted mass of aluminium, it's as mesmerizing as the museum's collection.

The impossible dream of a young architect, bankrolled by a billionaire, the Museo Soumaya has a story fit for the silver screen. In the early 2000s, Mexican entrepreneur Carlos Slim, then the world's wealthiest person, had a vision: to build a museum that would not only house his private collection but also serve as a gift to Mexico, helping Mexicans see world-class art without having to travel to Europe. It's thought that Slim's late wife, Soumaya Domit Gemayel, influenced his love for art and planted the seed of building a museum, and so it became a fitting tribute to her, too.

Keeping things in the family, Slim turned to his 35-year-old son-in-law, Fernando Romero, to design the building. The architect came up with an outlandish design that was dismissed by the media as being impossible to build – but it was nothing a whopping US$70 million couldn't make possible by 2011.

A DREAM COME TRUE

Asymmetrical, wide at the top and bottom and squeezed in the middle, the building resembles a spaceship being warped and squeezed as it passes through a wormhole. The aluminium coating, made up of 16,000 mirrored hexagons, reflects the bright lights and neon of downtown Mexico City; the mosaic finish, meanwhile, was designed as a modern take on the ceramic tiles that cover the city's colonial buildings. The burrow-like tunnel that serves as the way into the museum only adds to the feeling that this is no ordinary art gallery, with the cyberpunk shimmer of the exterior giving way to a cavernous world of softly lit white marble and light-wood floors.

The museum's unusual shape is utilized to give a lovely flow to the visitor experience. Over six floors, the galleries aren't separated by stairs and walls, but rather joined by sloping ramps that spiral up the inside of the building, reminiscent of New York City's Guggenheim Museum *(p188)*. Within these galleries are over 65,000 pieces spanning three millennia, including European masterpieces by Picasso and Monet. As you admire Slim's collection within walls that were once thought to be impossible to build, you can't help but feel that he achieved his vision: to give people world-class art in a world-class building.

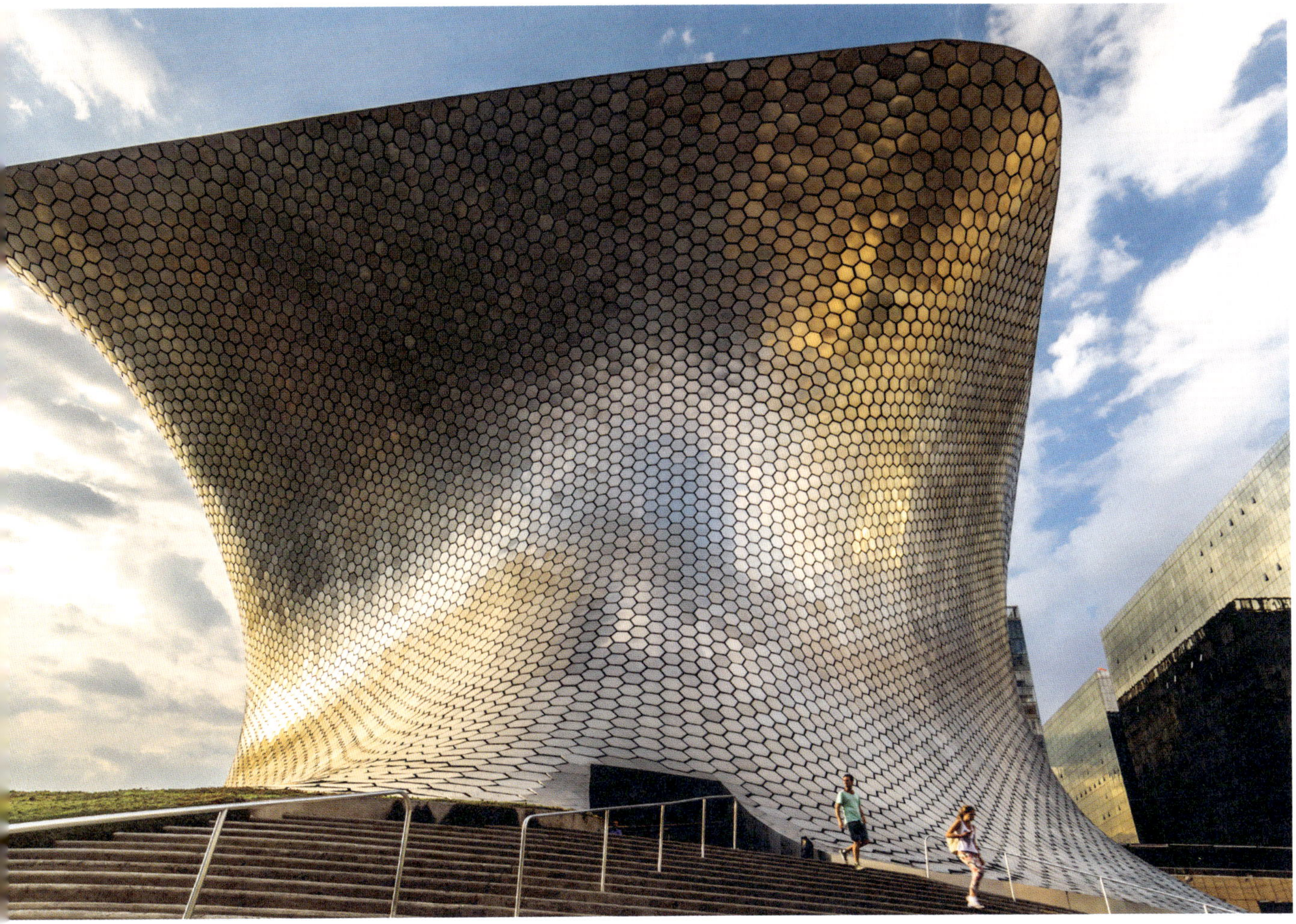

MORE LIKE THIS

Harbin Opera House, China
This sinuous building, designed by Beijing-based architecture firm MAD, has tentacle-like side buildings that make it look like it's slipped out of the Songhua River. The wood shell interior is just as dramatic.

Selfridges, UK
A cornerstone of Birmingham city centre's rejuvenation, this curving structure housing the Selfridges department store is covered in domed discs. It's intended to evoke both the curves of the female figure and a 1960s Paco Rabanne chain-mail dress design.

The Pyramid of the Moon, one of two huge pyramids in Teotihuacán

SAN JUAN TEOTIHUACÁN • MEXICO

TEOTIHUACÁN

WHERE Ave Pirámides, Purificacion **TRANSPORT** Buses leave every 15–30 mins from Mexico City's Terminal del Norte (Autobuses Teotihuacán) **INFORMATION** Open 8am–5pm daily (last entry: 4:30pm); tours run from Mexico City and include transport and admission to the site

If this was all that remained of your civilization centuries later, you wouldn't be too disappointed. Rivalling Mexico's more famous Chichén Itzá, the colossal ceremonial complex of Teotihuacán is epic.

Think the Aztecs are ancient? Think again. Established around 100 BCE, Teotihuacán is one of the most spectacular sites of the ancient world. It was founded long before the arrival of the Spanish and was already old and abandoned when the Aztecs arrived in the Valley of Mexico. In its prime, this huge urban centre may have housed up to 125,000 people and covered over 20 sq km (8 sq miles), dominating life in the region for 500 years before being destroyed and abandoned around 650 CE. The Aztecs named it "the place where men became gods", and it's easy to see why: though only ruins and a fraction of the site remain, even today it inspires awe. And we still know hardly anything about the Pre-Columbian civilization that created it.

CENTRE OF THE UNIVERSE

Strolling down the Avenue of the Dead, Teotihuacán's central spine, you'll immediately sense this was a site of incredible importance. You might make out temples and palaces perhaps, but there's little to deny the two hulking stepped pyramids, facing each other across a vast plaza like mini mountains. You'll see the Pyramid of the Sun long before you reach it: five sloping levels rising some 70 m (230 ft) into the sky. It's huge, containing around 2.5 million tonnes of stone and earth packed within its four symmetrical stone and adobe sides. You can't climb it, but you can climb its twin: the Pyramid of the Moon. Clamber up the steep stone stairs (you can only climb to the first level), a sweaty hike in the sun, and you'll be rewarded with a spectacular panorama of the whole site. As you survey it, you'll start to wonder: what was all this for? Some great tomb or monument to the dead? Temples and palaces for kings or queens? Some vast astronomical or solar calendar perhaps? Like the rest of Teotihuacán, the exact function of the buildings here remains unclear, though one thing is certain: whoever built this city, built to impress.

PHOTO OPPORTUNITY

For an unforgettable experience and sweeping view of the ancient remains, take a sunrise balloon ride over the site *(tlatoanitours mexico.com/tours/ balloonteotihuacan)*.

The Pyramid of Kulkulkán and the Great Ball Court

YUCATÁN • MEXICO

CHICHÉN ITZÁ

WHERE Off Highway 180, 42 km (26 miles) west of Valladolid **TRANSPORT** Buses run from major Yucatán towns and cities; tours run from Cancún **INFORMATION** Open 8am–5pm daily (last entry 4pm); Noches de Kulkulkán light show: 8pm Wed–Sun in summer, 7pm in winter; buy tickets online via a tour company to avoid long lines at the ticket booth

Steeped in mystery, the immense temples, pyramids and palaces of Chichén Itzá stand as a testament to the astonishing ingenuity and cultural richness of the ancient Maya.

Unanswered questions swirl around the ancient stones of Chichén Itzá. Some 1,200 years ago, this city in Mexico's lush, tropical Yucatán Peninsula rose to become the hub of a multicultural Mesoamerican superpower. So why was it later mysteriously, perhaps suddenly, abandoned? What scenes of bloodthirsty torture and sacrifice took place here? And who really built its awe-inspiring monuments? Chichén Itzá guards its secrets closely – part of the reason why this spectacular site holds such a powerful grip on the imagination.

BUILT TO IMPRESS

Chichén Itzá was no ordinary city. This sprawling site is believed to have been one of the largest Maya settlements in the world and its ruins are vast, with monuments dotted across 10 sq km (4 sq miles). Yet one building stands out. Dramatic in scale and perfect in precision, the city's grandest glory rises before you as soon as you step from the dappled entrance path onto the site's central grassy plaza. This is the Pyramid of Kulkulkán (also known as El Castillo), which towers 30 m (100 ft) high and features nine steep terraces climbing to a platform at its summit. It's more than just a marvel of ancient engineering, however. Dedicated to the serpent deity of Maya mythology, the temple is also a giant living calendar: on each of its four sides rise 91 steps, which, added to the top platform, make 365 – the number of days in the solar year.

Nearby, the Temple of the Warriors is almost as impressive, flanked on two sides by dozens of columns that stretch far into the distance. Carvings depict richly dressed warriors – evidence, some say, that this was a meeting place for the city's military elites to display their power. It had a ritual purpose, too. Look up and you'll spot a reclining figure

NORTH AMERICA   225

Above *Statue of the Mayan rain god Chac*

Right *One of the hoops on the Great Ball Court*

of the rain god Chac guarding the sanctuary atop; he holds a bowl thought to be for sacrificial offerings.

BLOOD SPORTS

More macabre scenes await across the plaza to the west. Here, a low platform (the Tzompantli) is etched with carvings of hundreds of grinning skulls – it's thought in Chichén Itzá's heyday the severed heads of the city's vanquished enemies were stacked on latticed wooden racks on top. The killings may have been carried out at the nearby Platform of the Eagles and Jaguars, where the ferocious beasts are depicted holding human hearts in their claws.

Enter the nearby Great Ball Court and things *seem* a little less grisly. Wider than a modern football pitch and almost twice as long, this immense site was the largest ever built in Mesoamerica. It was the setting for a somewhat extreme version of basketball, where points were scored by propelling a heavy rubber ball through the carved stone rings high on the court's towering walls. Sounds fun? Not for the losers: it's thought that the game had a ritual purpose beyond sport, and if you lost, you lost your head (literally).

SACRED WELL

Dozens more ruins await to the south, but before striking onwards, follow the sacbé

The green waters of the Sacred Cenote, a sinkhole steeped in myth

(Maya causeway) north to the Sacred Cenote, the largest of the four giant sinkholes that provided the city with its only surface water. Fringed by forest, it appears a peaceful, shaded spot for some reflection. To the Maya, this was a sacred portal to the underworld, guarded by Chac, and into its murky depths were thrown countless sacrificial offerings – objects in jade and gold, weapons and the bodies of at least 200 men, women and children. There's mounting evidence that severe drought may have caused cenote levels to plummet around the time of the city's decline. Were these offerings a desperate plea for rain? Chichén Itzá isn't ready to yield up its secrets just yet.

WHEN TO GO

Twice a year, at the spring and autumn equinoxes, thousands flock to El Castillo to witness the extraordinary Descent of Kulkulkán. Light and shadow create the illusion of a serpent writhing down the pyramid's northern balustrade, symbolizing the deity's return to earth. Cheers ring out when the sunlight reaches the stone serpents' heads at its base. An evening light show, staged throughout the year, recreates the effect.

NORTH AMERICA

SOUTH AMERICA

One site dominates the conversation when it comes to South America's architecture: Machu Picchu. This epic Inca citadel is arguably the continent's most famous building (or rather, series of buildings), and while it more than lives up to its fame, it's not the only draw here. South America's architecture is varied, to say the least. Some cities have been shaped by colonizers – look to Colombia's Cartagena – while others have been built from the ground up by iconic local architects, Brazil's capital being the most famous example. Add in dazzling religious monuments, creative art museums and stunning opera houses and you'll soon realize that, for a region long overlooked for its architecture, it certainly packs a punch.

CARTAGENA · COLOMBIA

CARTAGENA'S OLD TOWN

TRANSPORT Cartagena has a well-connected bus terminal and airport
INFORMATION Numerous companies run walking tours of the city

Cartagena is a tale of two cities. One is a modern metropolis of glassy skyscrapers, the other is a maze of historic buildings, draped with Bougainvillea and decorated with colourful murals. Can you guess where most tourists spend their time?

Cartagena's Old Town is an easy place to fall in love with. Walk its warren of cobblestone streets and you'll pass whitewashed churches, pretty palaces and ice cream-coloured mansions, their balconies draped with flowers. Leafy plazas and shady courtyards are also dotted around, and many alleyways are lined with gorgeous street art and buzzing with local bars and restaurants. It's beautiful at every turn – you'll find it hard not to take photos – but there's more here than meets the eye. Collectively, these buildings form one of the finest examples of colonial architecture in the Americas. In doing so, they offer not just a pretty face, but a window into Cartagena's story over the past five centuries.

A UNESCO World Heritage Site, this Caribbean port was founded by the Spanish in 1533 (though Indigenous peoples had long occupied the surrounding area). It quickly became a wealthy trading hub, and over the span of the 16th, 17th and 18th centuries, the Spanish built a series of grand buildings, many of which still stand today. The best way to learn their history? Take a guided walking tour (many are free, excluding a tip).

Before you enter the maze of the Old Town, you'll pass the mighty Castillo San Felipe de Barajas (largely built in the 17th century). Occupying a hilltop vantage point, this impregnable fortress – along with the city's fortified walls – was built to defend Cartagena against pirate raids and naval assaults. But not before a certain English privateer-pirate, Francis Drake, attacked in 1586 – once in the Old Town, look closely at the Catedral de Santa Catalina de Alejandría and you'll see the scars of Drake's fierce bombardments. A short walk from the cathedral, more history awaits: the triangular Plaza de los Coches was once a market area in which enslaved people were bought and sold (one of the reasons the city grew so wealthy); today its colourful arches bustle with local vendors.

And there's so much more to discover. As you wander around this Caribbean port, be sure to look beyond the kaleidoscopic façades: history hides down every corner in Cartagena.

MUST-SEE BUILDINGS

BASILICA SANTA CATALINA DE ALEJANDRÍA
Work started on this yellow-tinted church in 1575, but it was badly damaged by Francis Drake's attack 11 years later. The building was eventually completed in 1612 and is famed for its domed tower that gazes across the Old Town *(Calle de los Santos de Piedra)*.

PALACIO DE LA INQUISICIÓN
Around 800 people were publicly executed for "heresy" in this stately Baroque building, before Spanish colonial rule was ended in 1821 *(Plaza de Bolivar Carrera 3 33)*.

PUERTA DE RELOJ
This triple-arched yellow gateway provides a suitably monumental entrance to the Old Town.

Clockwise from top left
The Puerta de Reloj, an entrance to the Old Town; the Basilica Santa Catalina de Alejandría's tower; historic Plaza de los Coches

The fairytale church, built across a gorge

IPIALES · COLOMBIA

SANTUARIO DE LAS LAJAS

WHERE Vía Ipiales–Potosí, 7 km (4 miles) from Ipiales **TRANSPORT** Shared taxis run from Ipiales bus terminal to Las Lajas (10 to 15 min) **INFORMATION** The church is open 5am–7pm daily; entry is free (laslajas.org)

Is it a medieval mirage? Some sort of fantasy inspired by *Lord of the Rings*? Few sights are more unexpected than the Santuario de Las Lajas, a dazzling French Gothic basilica perched in a gorge high in the Colombian Andes.

Legends swirl around this fantastical church, but the most popular story goes like this. One dark stormy night in 1754, María Mueses de Quiñónez, a local Indigenous woman, and her deaf-mute daughter Rosa were sheltering from the rain in a remote canyon when, suddenly, a painted image of the Virgin Mary appeared on the rocks. Upon seeing it, Rosa was miraculously able to speak for the first time. Word of the event quickly spread, and soon the faithful began reporting other miracles at the site. As a result, a simple shrine was built to protect the image. In later years, this was replaced with a stone structure, built in the Spanish colonial style, but by the 1890s, the faithful decided they needed something more spectacular.

A FRENCH GOTHIC FANTASY

Enter Ecuadorian engineer Gualberto Pérez and local architect Lucindo Espinosa, who were chosen to build the church. Before they got started, they had a choice to make: stick with a Spanish style or create something new. For context, in the late 19th and early 20th centuries the newly independent countries of South America (of which Colombia was one) were looking to emphasize their separation from Spain. With this in mind, Pérez and Espinosa decided to demolish the old Spanish church on site and start from scratch. Using a Gothic Revival style that mimicked cathedrals in France, they set about creating a fittingly magical structure for the miraculous image inside. Construction took 33 years (1916–1949) and was incredibly challenging: the pair had to work out how to build the multi-storey base and elegantly arched bridge some 50 m (160 ft) above the rushing river below, before even starting the church. And the church wasn't much simpler. Sporting delicate pinnacles, lofty spires and flying buttresses, this grey-and-white granite structure was a true labour of love. Its exterior and dramatic location are often the highlights for visitors – few churches look like *this* – but the interior is the main focus for the faithful. Fibreglass mosaics and brilliant stained-glass windows are little distraction to those pilgrims who travel all the way to this remote region to see the altar, adorned with the same painted image of the Virgin Mary that appeared all those years ago.

SOUTH AMERICA

Machu Picchu, constructed in the classical Inca style

95

CUSCO · PERU

MACHU PICCHU

WHERE 9 km (6 miles) southwest of Machu Picchu Pueblo, Urubamba **TRANSPORT** Machu Picchu Pueblo (train station), then bus or hike **INFORMATION** Open 6am–5:30pm; maximum visit time four hours; book six months in advance (ticketmachupicchu.com)

Machu Picchu is, arguably, the most famous sight in all of South America. Perched on a precipitous ridge in the heart of the Andes, this epic Inca Empire citadel is on everyone's bucket list.

Reaching Machu Picchu is no small feat. This ancient Inca complex is hidden deep in the Peruvian Andes, requiring a lengthy combination of buses and trains, or a multi-day hike if you'd prefer the scenic route, to get there. But whatever journey you take, the destination, in this case, is always worth it. Clinging to a jungle-fringed mountainside, this world-famous Inca citadel is a place befitting of superlatives. It's one of the greatest architectural achievements anywhere in the world – so impressive that it was deemed one of the "New Seven Wonders of the World" in 2007. Today, it's Peru's biggest tourism draw (whether you arrive early or late in the day, or during the on-season or the off-season, you'll always be accompanied by a crowd).

ANCIENT ARCHITECTURE

Few written records survive on the original construction of Machu Picchu, but historians and archaeologists have agreed on a few things. First of all: Machu Picchu was constructed by the ancient Inca civilization around 1420–1450 (by this point, the Incas had become Latin America's largest empire, ever). Second: Machu Picchu was likely built as a palatial residence for the Inca emperor Pachacuti Inca Yupanqui. And finally: the citadel was inhabited for around a century, before being abandoned and, for a long while, lost.

Why was it abandoned? Some say due to the threat of Spanish conquests in the area, others say due to diseases (likely introduced by those Spanish invaders). But while it's true the Spanish were in the area, amazingly, they never found Machu Picchu. And neither did anyone else – until the early 20th century, that is. As a result, these near-flawless, 600-year-old ruins remained incredibly well preserved, and today they offer a rare glimpse into pre-colonial Peru – and the master builders who once ruled the area.

Precisely cut and precisely placed Inca stonework

The Incas could hardly have found a trickier site to build Machu Picchu on. Sitting at an altitude of 2,350 m (7,710 ft), and flanked by sheer drops to the Urubamba Valley below, this stone-built citadel is a masterclass in engineering and architecture (the Incas were really just showing off). Gazing at this elaborate township, the first question you'll probably have is, how did an ancient civilization build a citadel on gradients many would struggle even to climb? Experts believe these nifty ancient architects used a combination of rollers, ropes and ramps to lug the huge stones up from nearby quarries; these stones were then precisely cut (using a technique called ashlar masonry) to fit together without the need for mortar – they're wedged so seamlessly that you couldn't even fit a card between them. While this building technique was favoured for its aesthetic value, it was also practical: during earthquakes the stones bounced a little but soon fell back into place; they were, essentially, earthquake-proof.

As you walk through the city, things only get more awe-inspiring. Comprising an upper and lower section with houses, temples, plazas and agricultural terraces, Machu Picchu is linked up by scores of neatly designed stairways and paths. It also sports a complex-wide fountain and canal network, which cleverly funnelled water from natural springs around the city.

Machu Picchu's diverse sights leave visitors with some tough choices. Do you go straight for the highlights, like the Temple of the Three Windows, with its trapezoidal design to allow observation of sunrise and sunset, or the Temple of the Sun, raised to make offerings to the Inca's most important god, Inti, and only entered by empire elite? Do you zone in on compelling smaller details, like Intihuatana, the sundial-like "Hitching Post of the Sun" that determined agricultural cycles? Or do you clamber the site's picturesque peaks, Huayna Picchu or Machu Picchu Mountain, for some of the most impressive panoramas in the Andes? Whatever your choice, one thing is true: you won't be disappointed.

WHEN TO GO

Visit between April and October, the Andean dry season, when the site is less muddy and less likely to be cloud-covered. The special Inti Raymi in Cusco, a festival honouring the sun, is held on 24 June.

Left The Intihuatana stone, used as a sundial

Above The curving terraces of the citadel, built atop a mountain

Right Pretty in pink, the belle-époque exterior of the theatre

Below Opulence overload in the main hall

MANAUS · BRAZIL

TEATRO AMAZONAS

WHERE Largo de São Sebastião **TRANSPORT** The nearest bus stop is Estação de Transferência 2; you can fly or take the ferry into Manaus **INFORMATION** Tours run 10am–5pm daily; performances take place regularly (head inside for details)

The middle of the Amazon rainforest might seem an unlikely location for a great, gleaming opera house, but that's what makes the Amazon Theatre so enchanting. Meet the miracle of Manaus.

Manaus is a marvel in itself. Located deep in the jungle, on the banks of the Rio Negro, this modern city is a whopping 1,400 km (870 miles) from the ocean, yet it's home to the largest floating port in the world. It witnessed a brief economic boom in the 19th century, thanks to the export of rubber, and its riches were quickly funnelled into grand building projects – none grander than the Teatro Amazonas.

OPERA IN THE AMAZON

The Amazon Theatre was built during the belle époque era, when European style was the height of fashion in colonial South America. Buoyant from the rubber boom, the city spared no expense when following the trend: Venetian glass, Alsatian roof tiles and Carrara marble were shipped in, as was an Italian artist, who painted the ceiling's dome to resemble an impression of the Eiffel Tower seen from beneath. The result? A giant, mosaiced cupcake of a building that glitters in the tropical sun. It's a beauty, but the first thing you'll notice is its sheer size, looming above the surrounding buildings at 92 m (302 ft) high. Its auditorium seats more than 700 people and is illuminated by 198 Italian chandeliers, while the glittering dome, decked out in the yellow and green of the Brazilian flag, is adorned with 36,000 ceramic tiles. The dome rises from a pyramidal roof, deep red and resembling one side of a cut ruby – fitting, given that the building was first imagined by local politician Antonio Jose Fernandes Júnior as a "jewel" in the heart of the jungle.

Catching a performance here feels a little surreal – you are, after all, very, very deep in the jungle. But if there's nothing on, don't worry. Guided tours are on hand to usher you up the opulent Carrara marble staircases and past the Scottish cast-iron columns, built hollow for the best acoustics. Because here, the sound of the rainforest is music, not birdsong.

MORE LIKE THIS

Palais Garnier, France
Few buildings epitomize the belle époque quite like this Parisian opera house. So opulent was the building (picture gold upon gold upon gold) that it became known as a palace, rather than simply an opera house.

Teatro Colón, Argentina
Built in the mid-19th century and refurbished in the early 21st century, Buenos Aires' opera house is beloved by performers for its top-notch acoustics. Patrons will be more enamoured by the design – look up at the gorgeous hand-painted dome.

Brasília's unusual cathedral, most of which is underground

97

BRASÍLIA · BRAZIL

BRASÍLIA

WHERE Niemeyer's civic buildings can be found in the city's core
TRANSPORT The nearest train station is Federal District Metro

A peaceful counterpoint to the carnivalesque chaos of Brazil's other big cities, the country's capital feels neat, formal and calm. It was planned that way, and its buildings (the work of master Modernist Oscar Niemeyer) fit right in.

Some cities grow gradually, beginning as tiny hamlets, old fishing villages or ancient settlements and rising into modern metropolises over the course of centuries (or even millennia). Not Brasília. Construction of Brazil's famous planned city began in 1956, and just a few years later the city was inaugurated as the country's new capital in 1960. But while Brasília is officially a baby boomer, plans for the capital began a lot earlier than the 1950s.

Legend speaks of an Italian priest, Don Bosco, having a prophetic dream in 1883 of a brand-new, cutting-edge city popping up in the arid grasslands of the Cerrado (Brazil's tropical savanna), where Brasília is now. It's a fun story, but in reality, the city's origins are down to more practical reasons. As early as 1827, statesman José Bonifácio had proposed moving Brazil's capital from Rio de Janeiro to a new location inland, closer to the geographical centre of the country.

It wasn't until 1956, however, that the plans came to fruition. Having promised to develop Brazil's interior during his campaign, newly elected President Juscelino Kubitschek got to work on the new capital, swiftly assembling a team of city planners, designers and architects, led by chief architect Oscar Niemeyer. Together, they envisioned the capital as a modern utopia, designed to match Brazil's national motto, Ordem e Progresso (Order and Progress). With this in mind, the blueprint for the city was laid out on two axes – a horizontal one containing the civic buildings and a vertical one with residential properties – that formed the shape of an aeroplane. These functional zones were then broken up by manicured green belts (wide boulevards and grassy plazas) to soften the abundance of concrete. All in all, it was a masterclass in modern urban planning and part of the reason the city was listed as a UNESCO World Heritage Site. The other reason? The architecture.

MODERN MONUMENTS

Niemeyer realized his designs for the city at breakneck speed, but the result was far from slapdash. Brasília's civic buildings are minimalist and monumental, designed to create a feeling of choreographed calm, rather than the usual carefree chaos of Brazilian cities. Dotted around the city's core, Niemeyer's buildings loom above the neat green lawns with their mix of striking clean lines (in harmony with the flat landscape and a marker of mid-century modern) and geometric curves (the architect had a penchant for sculptural curves and UFO-like designs; p244). Most of them are crafted from reinforced concrete and clad in brilliant white, dazzling in the bright Brazilian sun and indicative of the optimism behind this futuristic utopia.

Each building will stop you in your tracks, but some are arguably better than others. The most spectacular? That title goes to the Roman Catholic Cathedral (or the Catedral Metropolitana Nossa Senhora Aparecida, to give it its full title). Niemeyer clearly threw tradition out the window when designing this one. Resembling a great glass-and-concrete onion, half-buried in the earth, the cathedral features 16 soaring curved pillars, held together at their apex by a high-tensile steel ring. Between the pillars are beautiful stained-glass windows, which become all the more apparent once you step inside. Or rather, once you *descend* inside. Most of the cathedral is actually subterranean – the crown-like structure visible from the ground is just the cathedral's roof. It's a strange feeling, walking into an underground church, but looking up towards the open "stem" of the roof from which statues of angels hang and light pours in, the whole effect is transcendent, almost heavenly. You might be surprised to hear that Niemeyer was a lifelong atheist.

Niemeyer's other masterworks in Brasília include the Praça dos Três Poderes, a square home to the city's most important, and striking, civic buildings. Brazil's National Congress sits in a sci-fi edifice with a central tower bookended by two bowl-like structures (one facing upwards and the other downwards), resembling giant satellite dishes. The president's official workplace, meanwhile, is the Palácio do Planalto, surrounded by clipped lawns and a reflecting pool, home to Japanese carp.

Even in this stately civic square, though, there's a human touch. An 8-m- (26-ft-) tall sculpture, Os Guerreiros (The Warriors) depicts two abstract, curving figures holding spears. It was designed to represent the thousands of architects, masons and construction workers on whose shoulders Brasília – this gleaming, utopian vision of Brazil's future – was built.

PHOTO OPPORTUNITY

For a bird's-eye view over Brasília, ascend the TV Tower (free to enter), which has a 75-m (246-ft) viewing platform looking straight down Jardim Burle Marx, a park in the middle of the vertical axis, the city's main central avenue.

Clockwise from left
The stained-glass interior of the city's cathedral; the National Congress building; the Palácio do Planalto

MUST-SEE BUILDINGS

ROMAN CATHOLIC CATHEDRAL
Arguably the highlight of Brasília, this Niemeyer masterpiece is flanked by bronze statues of Matthew, Mark, Luke and John *(Esplanada dos Ministérios)*.

NATIONAL CONGRESS
This government building is divided into an area for the Senate (under the cupola) and an area for the Chamber of Deputies, beneath the inverted dome *(Praça dos 3 Poderes)*.

TV TOWER
This glass-fronted tower features 224 m (735 ft) of latticed steel, tapering to a sharp point.

ITAMARATY PALACE
Brazil's foreign ministry is housed in this squat, striking building, with outer walls made up of arches reflected in a pool *(Plano Piloto)*.

SOUTH AMERICA 243

The art museum, scenically located on Niterói's coast

NITERÓI · BRAZIL

NITERÓI CONTEMPORARY ART MUSEUM

WHERE Mirante da Boa Viagem **TRANSPORT** The easiest way to reach the museum is by taxi **INFORMATION** Open 10am–6pm Tue–Sun; ticket required (visit.niteroi.br)

No, you haven't just stumbled across a brilliant white UFO levitating above Niterói's shoreline. Designed by Oscar Niemeyer, this futuristic art gallery confirms the Brazilian architect's genius.

You can't miss it. Perched on a headland overlooking the glittering Guanabara Bay, the Niterói Contemporary Art Museum has a prime position on the coast of Rio de Janeiro's neighbouring city, Niterói. And it sticks out like a sore thumb. Its sweeping white curves and glassy ribbon of windows make it more akin to a just touched-down *USS Enterprise* than the nearby apartment blocks. But this museum was never built to blend in. Inaugurated in 1996, the Niterói Contemporary Art Museum is home to over 1,000 artworks from the collection of Brazilian João Sattamini, yet it's far more famous for its association with another Brazilian: Oscar Niemeyer.

IN OSCAR'S ORBIT
Not only does this futuristic museum look like a UFO, it also appears to hover like one too. How? That's down to the thin stem supporting the museum's top-heavy cupola. Underneath, an 817-sq-m (8,794-sq-ft) mirror pool reflects the building's bulk, further adding to the illusion. The main access ramp – a looping red tractor beam spiralling up into the building – also seems to cheat gravity.

Follow the ramp and you'll discover that it's equally space-agey inside. Grey- and cream-coloured interiors create a blank canvas for the gallery's contemporary artwork, while sinuous ceilings and curving staircases never quite let you forget you're in the centre of a would-be spaceship.

And just as you would in space, you get a great view inside. The building's continuous convex window offers a 360-degree panorama over the bay, creating a tension between the artificial and natural worlds. Gaze out and you'll spot surfers catching waves on Icaraí Beach, and beyond, Rio's skyline dwarfed by the giant granite mass of Sugarloaf Mountain. It's a cityscape Niemeyer drew much inspiration from, and it's only fitting that it's the gallery's most beloved artwork.

Clockwise from left Vilaró's colourful creations; the sprawl of Casapueblo; a pool on one of the hotel's terraces

PUNTA BALLENA · URUGUAY

CASAPUEBLO

WHERE Mar Mediterraneo **TRANSPORT** Buses run from Punta del Este to Punta Ballena **INFORMATION** The museum is open 10am–sunset (casapueblo.com.uy); the hotel is open year-round (clubhotelcasapueblo.com)

Cascading down the cliffs, the flamboyant Casapueblo is an artist home like no other. While it's an homage to one of Uruguay's biggest and brightest personalities, it's also an icon in itself.

Artists' homes are often quirky, but few look like this one. Created by multidisciplinary Uruguayan artist Carlos Páez Vilaró, the whimsical Casapueblo tumbles down a hillside on the edge of the Atlantic Ocean. Its whitewashed sprawl features 13 floors, all melded together organically (there are few straight lines here) and topped with a motley mix of terraces, domes and finials. From afar, it looks more like a series of higgledy-piggledy houses, but get a little closer and you'll realize it's actually just one – one "house village", as its name translates.

MORE THAN A HOUSE

Was Casapueblo inspired by the architecture of the Greek islands? You might think so, but not according to Vilaró. Instead, the artist found his inspiration closer to home, in the asymmetrical domed nests of the hornero, a Uruguayan bird. Like the nests, Casapueblo shies away from straight lines, favouring a seemingly haphazard mass of organic shapes. And the building began very organically, too. In 1958, Casapueblo was no more than a shack (Vilaró's first atelier), made from wood he found along the coast. Gradually, over the course of 36 years, it developed into a more concrete workplace, as well as a summer home for the artist and his friends.

Today, it has even more strings to its bow. Now part-art museum, part-hotel, Casapueblo has grown into an icon of Uruguayan architecture, attracting visitors from all around the world. Some come to stay in the hotel (which features 72 apartments, all unique and all promising epic Atlantic views). Others come for the museum, which features five rooms packed with Vilaró's art and sculptures (which ooze bold colours and nod to Afro-Uruguayan culture, about which he was passionate). But if you really want to get inside the mind of the artist, simply take a walk around the complex. This undulating labyrinthine layout is, you could say, as complex and unpredictable as Vilaró himself.

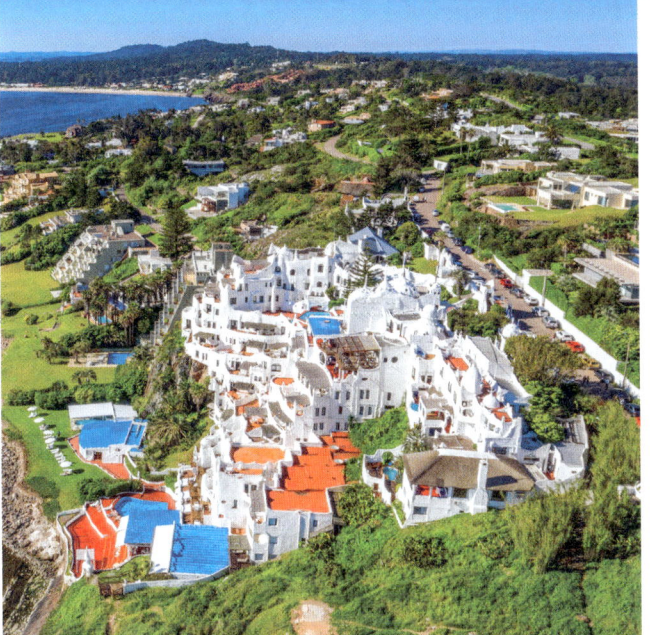

WHEN TO GO

Every evening, just before sunset, a recording of Carlos Páez Vilaró reading a poem to his friend is played around the hotel. The event is called the "Ceremony in the Sun" and makes for an atmospheric conclusion to the day.

SANTIAGO • CHILE

BAHÁ'Í TEMPLE OF SOUTH AMERICA

WHERE Ave Diagonal Las Torres 2000, Peñalolén
TRANSPORT The nearest metro station is Grecia, or take the bus at Ave Diagonal Las Torres **INFORMATION** Open 9am–6pm Tue–Sun; entry is free

The Bahá'í Temple of South America evokes many things – a wasps' nest, a lost jellyfish, a flower about to bloom. This may just be the most visually striking of the world's 13 Bahá'í temples. And that's saying something.

Every Bahá'í temple is different, and every Bahá'í temple is beautiful, but this one... this one takes the cake. Located just outside the Chilean capital of Santiago, this contemporary house of worship seems to appear out of nowhere, a little spaceship dropped in the cocoa-coloured foothills of the Andes mountains. In fact, nothing about this building is accidental, quite the opposite in fact.

Bahá'í temples *(p118)* are all designed with certain principles in mind – they must be circular and nine-sided to reflect sacred Bahá'í numerology. Chile's temple follows the rules but adds a dash of character: it features nine arching "petals" (made of cast-glass cladding but resembling delicate rice paper), ringed by nine pathways with nine reflecting pools. Inside, the overwhelming feeling is warmth: the floors and walls are made of rich walnut wood, and the amphitheatre-like pews are decked out in soft, dark leather. In keeping with all Bahá'í temples, the seats face no altar, and there is no formal liturgy beyond simple readings. Whatever your religion, you'll feel welcome here – the Bahá'í faith teaches tolerance, and you may well hear readings from the books of Hinduism, Buddhism, Christianity and Islam, as well as from the Bahá'í scriptures themselves. And if you have no faith at all, it's still a wonderfully meditative place, both inside and out. The gardens shiver with swaying grasses, and their quiet pathways are lined with soap bark trees, icons of Andean conservation whose leaves and bark emanate a sweet, earthy scent. If you're going to visit a Bahá'í temple, make it this one.

WHEN TO GO

Visit in April or May during the Bahá'í festival of Ridvan, when celebrants gather at the temple for shared meals and singing. Visitors are welcome to join.

Left The illuminated temple resembling a lantern with its light reflecting in the nine surrounding pools

Below Translucent marble panels forming the interior wall

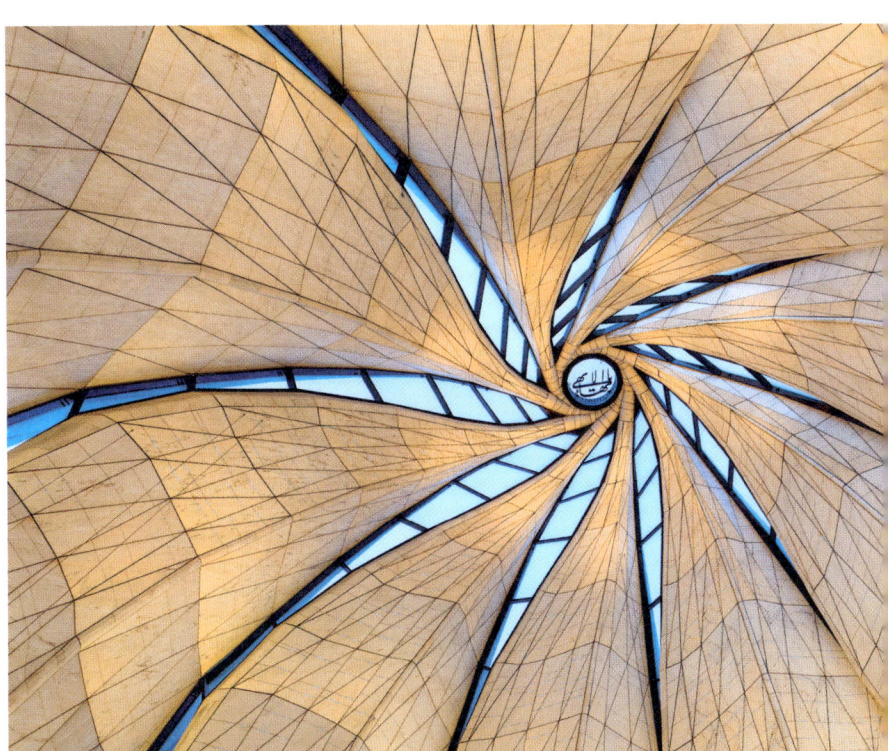

+ WHILE YOU'RE HERE

Most folks visiting the temple base themselves in Santiago proper, where a number of other architectural icons await. Take the Metropolitan Cathedral, an awesome Neo-Classical construction with bright biblical frescoes adorning the ceiling of its central nave. In contrast, the city is also home to the uber-modern Gran Torre Costanera, the tallest building in South America. This 300-m- (984-ft-) tall glass cylinder offers awesome views over Santiago from its 62nd-floor observation deck.

INDEX

A

Abadie, Paul 17
Accademia (Florence) 61
Aït Benhaddou (Drâa-Tafilalet) **88–9**
Alhambra (Granada) **30–31**
Amager Bakke (Copenhagen) **74–7**
Amboise, Château d' (France) 27
Amsterdam Canal District (Netherlands) **40–41**
Ancestral Puebloans 208–9
ancient monuments
    Angkor Wat (Siem Reap) 152–5, 162
    Chaco Culture National Historical Park (USA) 209
    Chichén Itzá (Mexico) 224–7
    Cliff Palace, Mesa Verde (USA) 208–9
    Colosseum (Rome) 50–53
    Machu Picchu (Peru) 234–7
    Taos Pueblo (USA) 209
    Tenochtitlan (Mexico) 217
    Teotihuacán (Mexico) 222–3
    see also pyramids; temples
Anis, Albert 213
Arch of Septimius Severus (Rome) 53
Argentina, Teatro Colón (Buenos Aires) 239
Art Deco 184–9, **210–13**
Art Nouveau 78–9, 211
Australia 166–75
Austria 25, 74–5
Ayutthaya Historical Park (Thailand) 155
Azerbaijan 112–3
Aztecs 222
azulejo tiles 38

B

Bagan (Mayanmar) 155
Bahá'í faith 118–19, **248–9**
Bahá'í Temple of South America (Chile) 248–9
Baitul Mukarram National Mosque (Dhaka) 151
Ban, Shigeru 175
Bangladesh 150–51
Banyon Temple (Siem Reap) 154
Baptistery (Florence) 61
Barcelona (Spain), Gaudí's **32–5**
Baroque 24, 25
Bartholdi, Frédéric Auguste 64, 182
Bartolotti House (Amsterdam) 41
Bath (UK), Georgian **12–13**
Baths of Caracalla (Rome) 53
Bauhaus Dessau **46–7**
belle époque 239
Bell Tower (Perth) **174–5**
Bernini, Gian Lorenzo 62
Boom-style buildings 170
Borobudur (Java) **163**
Botticelli, Sandro 60
Bourgeois, Louise, *Maman* 36, 37
Bradfield, John 167
Bran Castle (Romania) **67–9**
Brasília (Brazil) **240–43**
Brazil, Brasília 238–45
bridges 12, 13, 166–7, 202–3
Broniewski, Władysław 47
Brumidi, Constantino 192
Brunelleschi, Filippo 55, 59, 60
Budapest (Hungary), Art Nouveau **78–9**
Buddhism 144–7, 153, 156, 163
Bunjil Place (Melbourne) 172–3
Burj Al Arab (Dubai) 161
Burj Khalifa (Dubai) 105, **108–9**, 159
Butler, Kathleen 167
Byzantine style 42, 56–7, 72–3, 100

C

Caldoches people 178
Calligraphy, Islamic 115, 124
Cambodia 152–5, 162
Campanile (Venice) 56
Canada 214–17
Canal District (Amsterdam) **40–41**
Capitman, Barbara 211, 212
Capitol Complex (Chandigarh) 116
Carbon neutrality 75, 214
Cardboard Cathedral (Christchurch) **175–7**
Carlson, Edward 200
Cartagena (Columbia), Old Town **230–31**
Casa Batlló (Barcelona) 35
Casa del Guarda (Barcelona) 34
Casa Grande (Hearst Castle) 204
Casa Vicens (Barcelona) 34, 35
Casapueblo (Punta Ballena) **246–7**
castles and fortifications
    Bran Castle (Romania) 67–9
    Castillo San Felipe de Barajas (Cartagena) 230
    Great Wall of China 136–7
    Himeji Castle (Japan) 148–9
    Hwaeseong Fortress (Suwon) 143
    Ksar of Aït Benhaddou (Drâa-Tafilalet) 88–9
    Mehrangarh Fort (Jodhpur) 120–21
castles and fortifications (cont.)
    Neuschwanstein Castle (Germany) 42–3
    Walls of Marrakesh (Morocco) 87
    see also châteaux; palaces
Chaco Culture National Historical Park (USA) 209
Chambord, Château de (France) 27
Chandigarh (India) **118–19**
Changgyeonggung Palace (Seoul) 143
Château Frontenac (Québec) **214–15**
Châteauesque 214
châteaux of the Loire Valley (France) **26–7**
Chenonceau, Château de (France) 27
Chicago School **198–9**
Chichén Itzá (Mexico) **224–7**
Chile 248–9
China 113, 133–41
Chion-in (Kyoto) 147
churches and cathedrals
    Basilica di Santa Maria Novella (Florence) 60
    Cardboard Cathedral (Christchurch) 175–7
    Catedral de Santa Catalina de Alejandria (Cartagena) 230–31
    Catedral Metropolitana Nossa Senhora Aparecida (Brasília) 242, 243
    Church of Saint Sava (Belgrade) 63
    Duomo (Milan) 64–5
    Duomo of Santa Maria del Fiore (Florence) 55, 58–9, 60, 61
    Hagia Sophia (Istanbul) **72–3**
    Hallgrímskirkja (Reykjavik) 80–81
    Heddal Stave Church (Norway) **80–83**
    Metropolitan Cathedral (Mexico City) 217–19
    Metropolitan Cathedral (Santiago de Chile) 249
    Mosque-Cathedral of Córdoba (Spain) 28–9
    Notre-Dame Cathedral of Paris 20–21
    Pantheon (Rome) 54–5
    Sacré-Cœur (Paris) 17–19
    Sagrada Familia (Barcelona) 32–4, 35
churches and cathedrals (cont.)
    Santuario de Las Lajas (Colombia) 232–3
    St Mark's Basilica (Venice) 56–7
    St Paul's Cathedral (London) 63
    St Peter's (Rome) 62–3
Churrigueresque 217
Circus, The (Bath) 13
civic buildings
    Capitol Complex (Chandigarh) 116
    High Court of Punjab and Haryana (Chandigarh) 116–17
    Itamaraty Palace (Brasília) 243
    National Assembly Building (Dhaka) 150–51
    National Congress (Brasília) 242, 243
    Palace of Westminster (London) 14–15
    Parliament House (Melbourne) 170, 171
    US Capitol (Washington, DC) 191, 192, 193
    US Supreme Court (Washington, DC) 192, 193
Cliff Palace, Mesa Verde (USA) **208–9**
CN Tower (Toronto) **216–17**
Colombia 230–33
Colonial architecture 230–31
Colosseum (Rome) **50–53**
concert halls *see* entertainment venues
Court of Lions (Alhambra) 30, 31
Cubism 211
Curzon Hall (Dhaka) 151

D

Deconstructivism 189
Denmark 74–7
Deoksugung Palace (Seoul) 143
Diotisalvi 66
Dixon, L Murray 212
domes 54–5, 55, 56, 58–9, 60, 62, 63, 72, 103, 104–5
Donatello 59, 60
Doric columns 70
Dorman Long & Co. 167
Drew, Jane 116
Duomo (Milan) **64–5**
Dusit Maha Prasat (Grand Palace, Bangkok) 156

E

Egypt 94–9
Eiffel, Gustave 182

Eiffel Tower (Paris) **22–3**
Elbphilharmonie (Hamburg) **44–5**
Elizabeth Tower (Big Ben) (London) 14
Empire State Building (New York City) **184–7**
entertainment venues
    Colosseum (Rome) 50–53
    Elbphilharmonie (Hamburg) 44–5
    Guangzhou Opera House (China) 113
    Harbin Opera House (China) 221
    Heydar Aliyev Centre (Baku) 112–13
    Jay Pritzker Pavilion (Chicago) 207
    Jean-Marie Tjibaou Cultural Centre (Nouméa) **178–9**
    McCaw Hall (Seattle) 200
    Palace of Culture and Science (Warsaw) 47
    Palais Garnier (Paris) 239
    Petronas Towers (Kuala Lumpur) 159
    Sydney Opera House 166, 168–9
    Teatro Amazonas (Manaus) 238–9
    Walt Disney Concert Hall (Los Angeles) 206–7
Espinosa, Lucindo 233
Exhibition Building (Melbourne) 170, 171

F

Fallingwater (Pennsylvania) **195–7**
Ferdinand II of Portugal 38
First Nation Australians 172
Flinders Street Station (Melbourne) 170, 171
Florence (Italy), Renaissance 55, **58–61**
Fondation Louis Vuitton (Paris) 189
Forbidden City (Beijing) **138–41**
Forum (Rome) 53
France 17–27, 189, 239
France, Roy F 213
French Gothic 233
French Renaissance 214
Fry, Maxwell 116

G

Gang, Jeanne 189
Gateway Arch (St. Louis) **194–5**
Gaudí, Antoni **32–5**

Gehry, Frank 36, 161, 189, 202, 206–7
Gensler 133
Georgian architecture, Bath (UK) **12–13**
Germany 25, 42–7
Gilder Center for Science, Education and Innovation (New York City) 189
Ginkaku-ji (Kyoto) 146, 147
Giza, Pyramids of (Egypt) **84–5**
Golden Gate Bridge (San Francisco) **202–3**
Golden Temple of Amritsar (India) **128–9**
Gothic architecture 21, 64–5, 67–9, 214
Gothic Revival 14, 233
Grand Palace (Bangkok) **156–7**
Gran Torre Costanera (Santiago de Chile) 249
Great Hypostyle Hall (Karnak) 98
Great Mosque of Córdoba (Spain) **28–9**
Great Pyramid (Giza) 94–7
Great Wall of China **136–7**
Greece 70–71
Greek architecture 70–71
Greek Revival 190, 192
Gropius, Walter 46
Guangzhou Opera House (China) 113
Güell, Eusebi 34
Guggenheim Museum (Bilbao) **36–7**
Guggenheim Museum (New York City) **188–9**, 220
Guggenheim, Solomon R 36
Gwathmey Siegel 188
Gyeongbokgung Palace (Seoul) **142–3**

H

Hadid, Zaha 112, 113
Hagia Sophia (Istanbul) **72–3**
Hallgrímskirkja (Reykjavik) **80–81**
Hall of Mirrors (Versailles) 24
Hall of Supreme Harmony (Forbidden City) 140
Harbin Opera House (China) 221
Hearst Castle (California) **204–5**
Hearst, William Randolph 204
Heddal Stave Church (Norway) **80–83**
Herzog & de Meuron 44
Heydar Aliyev Centre (Baku) **112–13**

High Court of Punjab and Haryana (Chandigarh) 116, 117
High Place of Sacrifice (Petra) 100
Himeji Castle (Japan) **148–9**
Hinduism 126–7, 130–31, 153, 154, 162, 163
Hoban, James 192
Hohauser, Henry 212, 213
Hohenschwangau (Germany) 42–3
Horowitz, Leonard 212
hotels
    Avalon (Miami) 213
    Breakwater (Miami) 213
    Burj Al Arab (Dubai) 161
    Cavalier Hotel (Miami) 213
    Château Frontenac (Québec) 214–15
    Congress Hotel (Miami) 213
    Marina Bay Sands (Singapore) 160–61
    Marlin Hotel (Miami) 212
    Marqués de Riscal (Elciego) 161
    Tiffany Hotel (Miami) 212
    Waldorf Towers (Miami) 213
House of Commons (UK) 14
House of Lords (UK) 14
House of Tiberius (Rome) 53
Hungarian Geological Institute (Budapest) 79
Hungary 78–9
Hunt, Richard 182
Hwaeseong Fortress (Suwon) 143

I

Iceland 80–81
Inca 234–7
India 118–31
Indonesia 162–3
Intihuatana (Machu Picchu) 237
Islamic architecture/designs 108, 114–15, 122–5, 150, 159
Italy 50–67
Iznik tiles 73

J

Jainism 127
Japan 144–9
Java 162–3
Jay Pritzker Pavilion (Chicago) 207
Jean-Marie Tjibaou Cultural Centre (Nouméa) **178–9**
Jemaa-el-Fna (Marrakesh) 86–7
Jodhpur (India) 120–21
Jordan 100–101
Joseon dynasty 142

K

Kahn, Louis 150
Kanak people 178
Karnak Temple Complex (Luxor) **98–9**
Khafre, Pyramid of 96
Khajuraho (India) **126–7**
Khmer Empire 153
Khufu, Pyramid of (Giza) 94–6
Kinkaku-ji (Kyoto) 146
Kiyomizu-dera (Kyoto) 147
Koons, Jeff, *Puppy* 36
Ksar of Aït Benhaddou (Drâa-Tafilalet) **88–9**
Kubitschek, Juscelino 241
Kulin nation 172
Kunsthaus Graz (Austria) **74–5**

L

La Pedrera (Casa Milà) (Barcelona) 34, 35
Langeais, Château de (France) 27
Le Corbusier 116
L'Enfant, Pierre Charles 190
Le Nôtre, André 24
Leaning Tower of Pisa (Italy) **66–7**
Lechner, Ödön 78, 79
Leonardo da Vinci 59, 60
libraries 112–13, 132–3, 170, 171, 178–9
Lincoln Memorial (Washington, DC) 192, 193
Loire Valley Châteaux (France) **26–7**
London Aquatics Centre (UK) 113
Lotus Temple (Bahá'i House of Worship) (New Delhi) **118–19**
Louis XIV of France 24
Louvre Abu Dhabi (UAE) **104–5**
Ludwig II of Bavaria 42

M

Machu Picchu (Peru) **234–7**
MAD 221
madrasas 114–15
Maktoum, Sheikh 105, 108
Malaysia 158–9
Manueline architecture 38
Mapungubwe Interpretation Centre (Limpopo) **90–91**
Marie, Queen consort of Romania 67
Marina Bay Sands (Singapore) **160–61**
Marqués de Riscal (Elciego) 161
Marrakesh (Morocco) 86–7
MAXXI (Rome) 113

Maya 224–7
Medici family 59
Medina of Marrakesh (Morocco) **86–7**
Mediterranean Revival 204
Meenakshi Temple (Madurai) **130–31**
Mehrangarh Fort (Jodhpur) **120–21**
Melbourne (Australia), Victorian **170–71**
Menkaure, Pyramid of (Giza) 96, 97
Meridian Gate (Forbidden City) 138–40
Metropolitan Cathedral (Mexico City) **217–19**
Metropolitan Cathedral (Santiago de Chile) 249
Mexico 217–27
Miami (USA), Art Deco **210–213**
Michelangelo 60, 62
Michelozzo 59
Milan Cathedral (Italy) **64–5**
Ming dynasty 136, 137
Mntambo, Nandipha 91
Modernism 116–17, 150–51, 188, 240–43
Mohammed bin Rashid Al
Monadnock Building (Chicago) 199
Monastery (Petra) 100
Moorish architecture 28–31, 34, 35, 38
Morgan, Julia 204
Morocco 86–9
Morrow, Irving F 202
mosaics 17, 56, 63, 72, 103, 115, 233
mosques
    Baitul Mukarram National Mosque (Dhaka) 151
    Great Mosque of Córdoba (Spain) 28–9
    Great Mosque of Samarra (Iraq) 108
    Hagia Sophia (Istanbul) **72–3**
    Koutoubia Mosque (Marrakesh) 87
    Sheikh Zayed Grand Mosque (Abu Dhabi) 102–3
    Sultan Ahmed Mosque (Istanbul) 73
Mueses de Quiñónez, María and Rosa 233
Muholi, Zanele 91
museums and galleries
    Accademia (Florence) 60
    Art Deco Museum and Welcome Center (Miami) 212

museums and galleries (cont.)
    Bauhaus Dessau (Germany) 46–7
    Fondation Louis Vuitton (Paris) 189
    Gilder Center for Science, Education and Innovation (New York City) 189
    Government Museum and Art Gallery (Chandigarh) 117
    Grachtenmuseum (Amsterdam) 41
    Guggenheim Museum (Bilbao) 36–7
    Guggenheim Museum (New York City) 188–9, 220
    Heydar Aliyev Centre (Baku) 112–13
    Holburne Museum (Bath) 13
    Kunsthaus Graz (Austria) 74–5
    Louvre Abu Dhabi (UAE) 104–5
    Mapungubwe Interpretation Centre (South Africa) 90–91
    MAXXI (Rome) 113
    Museo Soumaya (Mexico City) 220–21
    Museum of Applied Arts (Budapest) 79
    Museum of Pop Culture (MoPOP) (Seattle) 200
    Museum of the Future (Dubai) 104–7
    Museum van Loon (Amsterdam) 41
    National Portrait Gallery (NPG) (Washington, DC) 193
    Niterói Contemporary Art Museum (Brazil) 244–5
    Pacific Science Center (Seattle) 200
    Palace of Culture and Science (Warsaw) 47
    Petronas Towers science museum (Kuala Lumpur) 159
    Smithsonian American Art Museum (SAAM) (Washington, DC) 193
    Uffizi (Florence) 60, 61
    Weisman Art Museum (Minneapolis) 207
    Zeitz MOCAA (Cape Town) 91–3
MVRDV 132
Myanmar 155

N

Nabataeans 100
Nasrid dynasty 30
National Archives (Washington, DC) 193
National Assembly Building (Dhaka) **150–51**
Nazi regime 46
Neo-Classical style **190–93**, 217
Neo-Gothic 14
Netherlands 40–41
Neuschwanstein Castle (Germany) **42–3**
New Caledonia, Jean-Marie Tjibaou Cultural Centre (Nouméa) 178–9
new cities 116–17, 240–43
New Zealand 175–7
Niemeyer, Oscar 240–45
Niterói Contemporary Art Museum (Brazil) **244–5**
Norway 80–83
Notre-Dame Cathedral of Paris **20–21**
Nouvel, Jean 104

O

Ocean Drive (Miami) 210–211, 212
Open Hand Monument (Chandigarh) 116, 117

P

Pacetti, Camillo 64
Pachacuti Inca Yupanqui 234
palaces
    Alhambra (Granada) **30–31**
    Changgyeonggung Palace (Seoul) 143
    Deoksugung Palace (Seoul) 143
    Forbidden City (Beijing) 138–41
    Grand Palace (Bangkok) 156–7
    Gyeongbokgung Palace (Seoul) 142–3
    Palace of Culture and Science (Warsaw) **47–9**
    Palace of Domitian (Rome) 53
    Palace of the Assembly (Chandigarh) 116, 117
    Palace of Versailles (France) **24–5**
    Palace of Westminster (London) **14–15**
    Palacio de la Inquisición (Cartagena) 231
    Palacio del Partal (Alhambra) 30

palaces (cont.)
    Palazzo Medici Riccardi (Florence) 59, 61
    Palazzo Pitti (Florence) 59
    Palazzo Vecchio (Florence) 61
    Pena Palace (Sintra) **38–9**
    Royal Pavilion (Brighton) 39
    Schönbrunn Palace (Vienna) 25
    Zwinger Palace (Dresden) 25
    see also castles and fortifications; châteaux
Pala d'Oro (St Mark's Basilica) 56
Palatine Hill (Rome) 53
Pantheon (Rome) **54–5**
parks and gardens
    Boboli Gardens (Florence) 59
    Parade Gardens (Bath) 13
    Park Güell (Barcelona) 34, 35
Parliament (UK) 14
Parliament House (Melbourne) 170, 171
Parthenon (Athens) **70–71**
Pena Palace (Sintra) **38–9**
Pérez, Gualberto 233
Peru 234–7
Petra (Wadi Musa) **100–101**
Petronas Towers (Kuala Lumpur) **158–9**
Pétursson, Hallgrímur 80
Piano, Renzo 16, 178
Piazza San Marco (Venice) 56
Picasso, Pablo 36
Pier Sixty (New York City) 173
Pisa, Leaning Tower of (Italy) **66–7**
Plateresque 217
Platform of the Eagles and Jaguars (Chichén Itzá) 226
Poland 47–9
Portmeirion (Wales) **39**
Portugal 38–9
Postal Savings Bank (Budapest) 79
power plants 74–7
Prambanan (Indonesia) **162**
Price, Bruce 214
Puerta de Reloj (Cartagena) 231
Pultney Bridge (Bath) 12, 13
pyramids
    Pyramid of Kulkulkán (El Castillo) (Chichén Itzá) 225, 227
    Pyramid of the Moon (Teotihuacán) 222–3
    Pyramid of the Sun (Teotihuacán) 222
    Pyramids of Giza 94–7

Q

Qin Shi Huang, Emperor 136

R

Rama I of Thailand 156
Ramargibodi I of Ayutthaya 155
Ramses II, Pharaoh 99
Rao Jodha 121
Registan (Samarkand) **114–15**
Reliance Building (Chicago) 199
Renaissance architecture, Florence **58–61**
Rich, Peter 90
Roman architecture 50–55, 100
Romania 67–9
Romano-Byzantine style 17
Romero, Fernando 220
Royal Crescent (Bath) 13
Royal Exhibition Building (Melbourne) 170, 171
Royal Pavilion (Brighton) **39**

S

Saadian Tombs (Marrakesh) 86, 87
Saarinen, Eero 194
Sacré-Cœur (Paris) **17–19**
Sacred Cenote (Chihén Itzá) 227
Safdie, Moshe 160
Sagrada Familia (Barcelona) **32–4**, 35
Sahba, Fariborz 118
St Louis, MO (USA) 194–5
Samarkand (Uzbekistan) 114–15
Samúelsson, Guðjón 80
Santuario de Las Lajas (Colombia) **232–3**
Schönbrunn Palace (Vienna) 25
Seattle Center (Seattle) **200–201**
Selfridges (Birmingham) 221
Seoul (South Korea) 142–3
Serbia, Church of St Sava (Belgrade) 63
Setas de Sevilla (Seville) 173
Seville (Spain) 173
Shah Jahan, Emperor 122, 124–5
Shanghai Tower (China) **133–5**
Shard, The (London) **16**
Sheikh Zayed Grand Mosque (Abu Dhabi) **102–3**
Sher-Dor Madrasa (Samarkand) 114–15
Sikhism 128–9
Silk Road 115
Singapore 160–61
Singel (Amsterdam) 40
Skisiewicz, Anton 213
skyscrapers
    Burj Khalifa (Dubai) 105, **108–9**
    Chicago School 198

skyscrapers (cont.)
    Chrysler Building (New York City) 184
    Empire State Building (New York City) 184–7
    Gran Torre Costanera (Santiago de Chile) 249
    Monadnock Building (Chicago) 199
    Petronas Towers (Kuala Lumpur) 158–9
    Reliance Building (Chicago) 199
    Second Leitner Building (Chicago) 199
    Shanghai Tower (China) 133–5
    Shard, The (London) 16
    Sullivan Center (Chicago) 199
Slim, Carlos 220
Smith, Adrian 108
Socrates 70
Soumaya, Museo (Mexico City) **220–21**
South Africa 90–93
South Korea 142–3
Space Needle (Seattle) 200
Spain 28–35, 161, 173
Spanish Baroque 204–5
Sphinx (Giza) 96
sports facilities 74–7, 113, 226
St Mark's Basilica (Venice) **56–7**
St Peter's (Rome) **62–3**
stained glass 17, 33, 173–5, 233, 242
Stalinist style 47
State Library (Melbourne) 171
Statue of Liberty (New York City) **182–3**
Stoker, Bram 67
Streamline Moderne 212, 213
Sukhothai Historical Park (Thailand) 155
Sullivan Center (Chicago) 199
Sultan Ahmed Mosque (Istanbul) 73
Suryavarman II of the Khmer Empire 153
Sydney Harbour Bridge (Australia) **166–7**
Sydney Opera House (Australia) 166, **168–9**
Szecesszjó 78, 79
Szenes House (Budapest) 79

T

Taj Mahal (Agra) **122–5**
Taos Pueblo (USA) 209
Ta Prohm (Siem Reap) 154

Teatro Amazonas (Manaus) **238–9**
Teatro Colón (Buenos Aires) 239
temples
    Angkor Wat (Siem Reap) 152–5, 162
    Bahá'í Temple of South America (Chile) 248–9
    Banyon Temple (Siem Reap) 154
    Borobudur (Java) 163
    Chion-in (Kyoto) 147
    Ginkaku-ji (Kyoto) 146, 147
    Golden Temple of Amritsar (India) 128–9
    Hatshepsut Temple (Luxor) 99
    Karnak Temple Complex (Luxor) 98–9
    Khajuraho (India) 126–7
    Kinkaku-ji (Kyoto) 146
    Kiyomizu-dera (Kyoto) 147
    Lotus Temple (New Delhi) 118–19
    Luxor Temple (Egypt) 99
    Meenakshi Temple (India) 130–31
    Pantheon (Rome) 54–5
    Parthenon (Athens) 70–71
    Prambanan (Indonesia) 162
    Ta Prohm (Siem Reap) 154
    Temple of Amun (Karnak) 98
    Temple of Saturn (Rome) 53
    Temple of the Sun (Machu Picchu) 237
    Temple of the Three Windows (Machu Picchu) 237
    Temple of the Warriors (Chichén Itzá) 225–6
    Temples of Kyoto (Japan) **144–7**
    Templo Mayor (Mexico City) 217
    Tenryu-ji (Kyoto) 147
    Teotihuacán (Mexico) 222
    To-ji (Kyoto) 144, 147
    Wat Phra Kaew (Bangkok) 156
Tenochtitlan (Mexico) 217
Tenryu-ji (Kyoto) 147
Teotihuacán (Mexico) **222–3**
Thailand 155–7
Tianjin Binhai Library (China) **132–3**
Tianjin Urban and Design Institute (China) 132
Tilya Kori Madrasa (Samarkand) 114–15
Timurid Renaissance 115
Tjibaou, Jean-Marie 178
To-ji (Kyoto) 144
tombs 86, 87, 122–5
    see also pyramids

Toronto (Canada) 216–17
Tower of the Shadow (Chandigarh) 117
Treasury (Petra) 100, 101
Tropical/Miami Deco 212, 213
Turkey 72–3
TV Tower (Brasília) 242, 243

U

UAE 102–7, 108–9, 161
Uffizi (Florence) 60, 61
Ulugh Beg Madrasa (Samarkand) 114–15
United Kingdom 12–16, 63, 113, 221
Uruguay 246–7
US Capitol (Washington, DC) 191, 192, 193
US Supreme Court (Washington, DC) 192, 193
USA 182–213
Utzon, Jørn 168
Uzbekistan 114–15

V

Van Horne, William 214
Vatican City 62
Victorian architecture 170–71
Vilaró, Carlos Páez 246–7
Visconti, Gian Galeazzo, Duke of Milan 64

W

Wales 39
Walt Disney Concert Hall (Los Angeles) **206–7**
Washington DC, Neo-Classical style **190–93**
Wat Phra Kaew (Bangkok) 156
Weisman Art Museum (Minneapolis) 207
Westminster Hall (London) 14
White House (Washington, DC) 192, 193
Willet-Holthuysen House (Amsterdam) 41
Wood, John the Elder and Younger 12, 13
Wren, Christopher 63
Wright, Frank Lloyd 188, 195–7

Y

Yoshimasa, Shogun 146, 147

Z

Zeitz MOCAA (Cape Town) **91–3**
Zen Buddhism 144–6
Zwinger Palace (Dresden) 25

ACKNOWLEDGMENTS

DK Travel would like to thank the following people for their contributions to this project:

EDWARD AVES has authored or contributed to more than 20 travel books, including guides to India, Sri Lanka and Laos as well as his native London. Passionate about architecture, he's also an avid hiker and when not sitting behind a desk is out exploring the UK's long-distance trails.

KIKI DEERE is an Anglo-Italian travel writer specializing in all things Italy. You'll likely find her swooshing down the pistes of the Dolomites, tucking into Italian fare at a family-run trattoria or reviewing the latest hotel opening on the Lakes. She regularly contributes to *The Telegraph*.

EMMA GREGG is an award-winning, UK-based travel journalist and author who has visited all seven continents. Of the seven, it's Africa that keeps calling her back. Specializing in nature, culture and sustainability, Emma has spent time in more than 30 African countries, sampling everything from high-end safaris to quirky folk festivals.

STEPHEN KEELING is a New York-based travel writer who has worked on numerous titles for DK Travel, including the award-winning *DK New York City* guide. His favourite building is the House in the Clouds in Suffolk, where he grew up.

JESSICA LEE is a Middle East-based travel writer and guidebook author who has lived in the region since 2007. She has authored over 30 travel guidebooks and her writing has appeared in *National Geographic Traveller*, *BBC Travel*, *The Telegraph*, *The Independent* and *Afar Magazine*.

DAPHNÉ LEPRINCE-RINGUET is a French journalist based in Paris. A tech reporter by day and a travel writer by night, she's a regular travel book contributor, with a special penchant for Brittany.

DAVID MASELLO writes about art, culture and architecture from New York City, where he has lived for more than 40 years. He's written three books about art and architecture, and many of his one-act plays have been performed by theatre companies in New York and Los Angeles. He is currently Executive Editor of *Milieu* magazine and Editor in Chief of *Art & Antiques* magazine.

SHAFIK MEGHJI is an award-winning journalist and travel writer based in south London. A Latin America specialist, he is the author of *Crossed Off the Map: Travels in Bolivia* and *Small Earthquakes: A Journey Through Lost British History in South America*. His bylines include *BBC Travel*, *National Geographic Traveller* and *Wanderlust*.

THOMAS O'MALLEY is a travel writer specializing in China, where he lived for 12 years. He is a regular guidebook author, covering the wider East Asia region, and reports on travel for *The Telegraph*. He once ate a banquet prepared by Chairman Mao's former chef.

ALEX RENNIE has worked on several titles for DK Travel and written for Atlas Obscura, *Resident Advisor* and *The Berliner*. Having semi-retired his dancing shoes, these days you'll find him roaming bookshops in Berlin (where he now lives), down by the lido or getting inspired by the magic of travel.

DANIEL STABLES is a travel writer for *National Geographic* and the BBC, and the author of *Fiesta: A Journey Through Festivity*. Raised in the West Country and based in Manchester, he can often be found toiling on the UK's long-distance walking trails and exploring festivals, folk rituals and obscure subcultures, at home and far away.

LUKE WATERSON is a Wales-based adventure, history and food travel writer. His obsession with ancient history has seen him researching prehistoric stone circles in the Orkney Islands for *Britain* magazine and Inca fortresses in South America for various travel guides.

ABOUT THE ILLUSTRATOR:

MARIA FEDOSEEVA is an award-winning illustrator and vector artist based in Berlin. Trained in type design, she brings a precise sensitivity to form and rhythm. A frequent traveller with a deep admiration for architecture, she drew on diverse structures and spaces to craft the book's illustrations.

The publisher would like to thank the following for their kind permission to reproduce their photographs:

(Key: a-above; b-below/bottom; c-centre; f-far; l-left; r-right; t-top)

123RF.com: Cristicroitoru 145; Gary Tog 231tl.

4Corners: Antonino Bartuccio 183; Francesco Carovillano 37tr, 37bc; Hans-Georg Eiben 27bl; Olimpio Fantuz 43cl; Günter Gräfenhain 237cr; Giuseppe Greco 53tr; Reinhard Schmid 71bc; Richard Taylor 168br; Luigi Vaccarella 66.

Adobe Stock: ABCDstock 137tr; Alexander 173; Aterrom 25tc; Auris 31tl; Bodia 152; Crazy nook 73tr; Davidzzzfr 79bc; Balate Dorin 66–69; Eyengel 169tc; Eyetronic 141tr; Farbregas1987 63tl; Alexey Fedorenko 13tr; Givaga 97cl; Ben Haskell 120; Helivideo 137tl; Heyengel 201cl; Ismael 37tl; Patrick Jennings 209tc; JossK 126br; Mapics 45; Conchi Martinez 199br; Mohamed 7; Muratart 123; New Travel Dreams 162tc; Nice 71tr; Nojo 9tl; Belikova Oksana 227cr; Onlyaphoto 13tl; Renatopmeireles 244; RH2010 58; SCStock 28bl, 89bc; Sforzza 61tl; Volodymyr Shevchuk 101; Arnav Pratap Singh 119bc; Stockbym 157bc, 161tc; Taiga 31bc, 39tl; Tichr 47; Whatafoto 99tr; Yasonya 41tc.

Alamy Stock Photo: Rubens Alarcon 35tr; Georg Berg 199tc; Martina Birnbaum 99br; Veaceslav Bordeianu 20; David Cherepuschak 126tc; Peter Cook VIEW 151bl; Ian Dagnall 65; Robert Harding 41bl; Hufton + Crow, courtesy of Zeitz MOCAA 92–93; Hufton+Crow-VIEW 76–77; Image Professionals GmbH 125cr, 247tl; ImageBROKER.com 201br; 237cl; Ivoha 82–83; Marco Trovalusci Photography 171tr; Conchi Martínez 199bl; Roberto Moiola 43tr; Nikreates 189tl; Obie Oberholzer / AfriPics 91bl; R Mac Photography 97br; RaRa 97tr; Sergi Reboredo 247bc; Galit Seligmann 117tl, 117tr; Sundry Photography 205br; Travelling Light 166bc; Travellinglight 139; Vibbily 169bl; Viennaslide 79tl, 79tr; Oliver Wintzen 239; Jan Wlodarczyk 86tc.

AWL Images: Alan Copson 16; Michele Falzone 124cl; Neil Farrin 28br; Gavin Hellier 13bc; Hemis 186tl; Karol Kozlowski 48–49, 71, 223, 247tl; Susanne Kremer 213tl; Stefano Politi Markovina 74br; Maurizio Rellini 41br, 53cl; Luigi Vaccarella 63tr.

Department of Culture and Tourism - Abu Dhabi: Department of Culture and Tourism - Abu Dhabi / Photo Hufton+Crow © 2025 Jean Nouvel / ADAGP, Paris and DACS, London 104–105tc; Department of Culture and Tourism – Abu Dhabi / Photo Mohamed Somji - Seeing Things © 2025 Jean Nouvel / ADAGP, Paris and DACS, London 104–105bc.

Dreamstime.com: Peter Adams 102br; Aguina 242; Bevanward 240; Blunker 235; Massimiliano Clari 102bl; Claudiodivizia 46; Cowardlion 132tr, 133bl; Cristim77 31tr; Dudljazov 171tl; Alexandre Fagundes De Fagundes 243tl; Patryk Kosmider 99bl; Jesse Kraft 236; Nicola Messana 114br; Saiko3p 117bc; Ivan Soto 25bl; Tifon Images 249tl, 249br; Noppasin Wongchum 158.

Emaar Properties PJSC: Emaar Properties PJSC 109.

Getty Images: Peter Adams 147bc, 155bc; Arctic Images 80tr; Kena Betancur 187br; Cavan Images 2; Michael Dunning 9tr; Grant Faint 141; Suyog Gaidhani 131tr; Pawel Gaul 32, 35tl, 213bc; Jeff Greenberg 221bc; Pascal Guyot / ADCK-CCT / Renzo Piano BW © DACS 2025 179; Richard I'Anson 174; Mathew Imaging 207tl; Mike Kline 194; Kulliprashant 131br; Shalender Kumar 129; Franz Marc Frei 209bc; Maremagnum 126bl; Mbell 193bc; Mtcurado 243bl; Jackal Pan 134–135; Paul Panayiotou 125cl; Chanachai Panichpattanakij 176–177; Sean Pavone Photo 147tl; Raspu 86br; Edwin Remsberg 73br; Manuel Romaris 226cl; Sylvain Sonnet 213tr; SvetlanaSF 61tr; Sam Swain 74tr; Urbancow 81bl; Emily M Wilson 114tr.

Getty Images / iStock: Avigator Photographer 9bc; Beijingstory 141br; Benedek 131cl, 203; Uwe Bergwitz 231bc; CBCK-Christine 166tc; Jorge Ivan Vasquez Cuartas 221tc; D. Lentz 147tr; Thomas Demarczyk 61bc; Emicristea 28tc; Espiegle 18–19; Diego Grandi 191; Gregobagel 201tr; July7th 143tc; KavalenkavaVolha 57; Makasana 86bl; Simon Mayer 231tr; Nicolas McComber 215; Mdmworks 216; Medvedkov 224; Anna Nelidova 95; Eloi Omella 51; Pgiam 207bc; Prakich 88br; Ni Qin 137bc; Rabbit75_ist 187bl; RCH Photo 232; RuslanKaln 113tc; Saiko3p 27br; SAKDAWUT14 155cl; Harpreet Singh 23; Tawanlubfah 157tr; YinYang 193tl; Vladislav Zolotov 27tc; Elena Zolotova 15.

Kate Hockenhull Photography: Kate Hockenhull 39tr.

Mark Holtzman/West Coast Aerial Photography; Inc: Mark Holtzman / West Coast Aerial Photography; Inc 205tc.

Peter Rich Architects: Peter Rich Architects / Obie Oberholzer 90tr.

Robert Harding Picture Library: Amanda Hall 187tr; Gavin Hellier 124cr; Greg Vaughn 157tl.

Shutterstock.com: Altrendo Images 239bc; Kiattisak Anoochitarom 4–5; Richie Chan 218–219; Alex Cimbal 173bc; Cornfield 155tr; Javier Catano Gonzalez 171bc; Diego Grandi 226cr; Marianna Ianovska 161bl; Jasmine K 63bc; Maxim Morales Lopez 35bc; Salvador Maniquiz 55br; Stefano Politi Markovina 204bl; MustakAhmedKafy 151tc; PhotoFires 25br; Posztos 113bl; Sakarin Sawasdinaka 149; Snap the frame 106–107; Stock for you 143bc; Vibgyor Studios 119tc; Huang Zheng 89bc.

Unsplash: Alain Bonnardeaux 162br; Nicholas Ceglia 189br; Gabriella Clare Marino 55tr; Yael Clusman 193tr; Yuhan Du 196–197; Christian Ladewig 185; Kevin Olson 102tc; Clark Van Der Beken 210.

Senior Editor Zoë Rutland
Project Editor Lucy Sara-Kelly
Senior Designer Katie Cavanagh
Project Art Editor Cristina Antequera
Designer Katie Thomas
Proofreader Clare Diston
Indexer Helen Peters
Picture Researcher Kate Hockenhull
Publishing Assistant Simona Velikova
Jacket and Sales Material Coordinator Serena Sclocco
Jacket Designers Cristina Antequera, Katie Thomas
Illustrator Maria Fedoseeva
Image Retoucher Tom Morse
Senior Production Editor Tony Phipps
Production Controller Kariss Ainsworth
Managing Art Editors Gemma Doyle, Michael Duffy
Editorial Director Hollie Teague
Art Director Maxine Pedliham
Publishing Director Georgina Dee

First published in Great Britain in 2026
by Dorling Kindersley Limited
20 Vauxhall Bridge Road,
London SW1V 2SA

The authorized representative in the EEA is
Dorling Kindersley Verlag GmbH. Arnulfstr. 124,
80636 Munich, Germany

Copyright © 2026 Dorling Kindersley Limited
A Penguin Random House Company
26 27 28 29 10 9 8 7 6 5 4 3 2 1
001–358002–Apr/2026

All rights reserved.
No part of this publication may be reproduced,
stored in or introduced into a retrieval system, or transmitted,
in any form, or by any means (electronic, mechanical, photocopying,
recording, or otherwise), without the
prior written permission of the copyright owner.

DK values and supports copyright. Thank you for respecting intellectual
property laws by not reproducing, scanning or distributing any part of
this publication by any means without permission. By purchasing an
authorised edition, you are supporting writers and artists and enabling
DK to continue
to publish books that inform and inspire readers.
No part of this publication may be used or reproduced in
any manner for the purpose of training artificial intelligence
technologies or systems. In accordance with Article 4(3)
of the DSM Directive 2019/790, DK expressly reserves this work from
the text and data mining exception.

A CIP catalogue record for this book
is available from the British Library.
ISBN: 978 0 2418 0157 4
Printed and bound in China

www.dk.com